TH
OF FAITH

THE PERSISTENCE OF FAITH

PHILIPPIANS 1 TO 4 / NORMAN PRITCHARD

AN ALBATROSS BOOK

the bible reading fellowship
OPENING THE BIBLE

© Commentary: Norman Pritchard 1993
© Discussion questions: Albatross Books Pty Ltd 1993

Published in Australia and New Zealand by
Albatross Books Pty Ltd
PO Box 320, Sutherland
NSW 2232, Australia
in the United States of America by
Albatross Books
PO Box 131, Claremont
CA 91711, USA
and in the United Kingdom by
Bible Reading Fellowship
Peter's Way, Sandy Lane West
Oxford OX4 5HG, England

First edition 1993

This book is copyright. Apart from any fair dealing for the purposes of private study, research, criticism or review as permitted under the Copyright Act, no part of this book may be reproduced by any process without the written permission of the publisher.

National Library of Australia
Cataloguing-in-Publication data

Pritchard, Norman
The Persistence of Faith

ISBN 0 86760 141 8 (Albatross)
ISBN 0 7459 2189 2 (Lion)

1. Bible. N.T. Philippians — Commentaries. I. Title

227.607

Cover photo: John Graham
Printed and bound in Australia by McPherson's Printing Group, Victoria

Contents

	Introduction	9
1	The prayer of faith *What difference does faith make?* PHILIPPIANS CHAPTER 1, VERSES 1 TO 11	21
2	The courage of faith *Can faith survive when up against it?* PHILIPPIANS CHAPTER 1, VERSES 12 TO 30	33
3	The best example of faith *How can we follow Jesus' example?* PHILIPPIANS CHAPTER 2, VERSES 1 TO 13	58
4	People of faith *How can we put faith into action?* PHILIPPIANS CHAPTER 2, VERSES 14 TO 30	81
5	Expressions of faith *What is the basis of our faith?* PHILIPPIANS CHAPTER 3, VERSES 1 TO 16	97

6 Faithful leadership
What is the goal of faith?
PHILIPPIANS CHAPTER 3, VERSES 17 TO 21
AND CHAPTER 4, VERSES 1 TO 4   122

7 The bonds of faith
What are the rewards of faith?
PHILIPPIANS CHAPTER 4, VERSES 4 TO 23   138
Endnotes   170
Bibliography   173

*To my mother
and in memory of my father,
with deep gratitude*

Introduction

WHEN WE READ ONE of the letters in the New Testament, we should never forget that we are reading someone else's mail. While it is true that some letters are actually essays dressed up in the form of letters — Hebrews, for example — most of the writings in the New Testament which we describe as letters originated as precisely that: pieces of correspondence, usually between an apostle and a church.

A letter for its time

Many of these letters are very specific — they are directed to a particular place, person or circumstance. The most obvious examples of this specific character occur in Paul's request for the cloak and books he had forgotten when writing in 2 Timothy 4, verse 13 and his advice to Timothy about his diet in 1 Timothy 5, verse 23.

The letter to the Philippians bears several unmistakable marks of having been written at a particular time and to particular people: there are references to what the author is doing as he writes 'what has happened to me' (chapter 1, verse 12), to his hopes for the future 'confident in the Lord, that I shall be coming myself before long' (chapter 2, verse 24), to what is going on in the relations between people in the church he writes to (chapter 4, verse 2) and so on.

It is also clear that the people to whom Paul is writing were particularly close to the apostle (Philippians 1, verse 3) and this gives the letter a very special place in the New Testament correspondence. We are able, by reading this letter, to sense something of the quality of relationships which could exist in the early church and to see Paul's need of support and gratitude for it as he blazed his missionary trail around the Mediterranean world. As biblical scholar Fred Craddock says: 'There is no indication that the writer or readers of Philippians ever thought it would be published, much less as sacred scripture! . . .As such it opens a window upon a relationship between the writer and the readers, a relationship which, by means of the letter, is remembered, enjoyed, nourished and informed.'[1]

The specific character of such a letter, however, also involves drawbacks. The letters in the New Testament were not necessarily written with a view to publication. They were written, as our letters are written, to bridge the gap created by absence and to give expression to the news and views, concerns and problems, which people who know each other share.

Because of this, the correspondents are able to presuppose knowledge of certain details to which we twentieth century readers are not privy. As a result, there are some sections of the letter which we cannot fully understand — for example, the identity of and circumstances surrounding the preachers who are making life difficult for Paul in chapter 1, verse 15. This is exactly as one would expect when reading someone else's mail, especially when the correspondents lived long ago and far away from us.

A letter for all time

This specific character, however, does not lock the letters away in some first-century filing cabinet, useful only for antiquarian interest. The letters of the early Christians were written as people sought to live the Christian faith and understand more fully how it required them to behave in their relationships with others, both in the church and in the world. Some of the questions which exercised people then appear in the letters, along with some of the answers which were given.

A mark of how seriously the early church took the gospel is the number of times a particular question is answered by reference to a gospel truth which more than transcends the original context of the question or problem. For example, the earliest record of what Jesus did at the Last Supper has been preserved in I Corinthians 11, verse 17 onwards because the church at Corinth experienced problems of disorder when the congregation met for worship.

The letter to the Philippians contains one classic example of this. In chapter 2, verses 1 to 13, when Paul feels the need to appeal for unity within the church, he grounds his appeal in a call for humility, which he advocates by reference to the 'mild, he lays his glory by' humility of Jesus — in coming to earth, suffering and dying for us. Most commentators believe that this passage contains the whole or part of an early Christian hymn — which would have been lost without trace, but for Paul's need to remind the church of the importance of humility. And while the original context of that lesson has passed, the lesson remains, and the profound way Paul taught that lesson has survived to guide and instruct us as we strive, in our very different day, to live out the gospel in our lives.

* * *

Although matters of critical scholarship are interesting and, in their own way, important, our understanding of Philippians is not affected over-much by the opinions we arrive at in relation to them. The two major critical questions surrounding Philippians concern the date the letter was written and the question of whether the text we have is the one letter Paul wrote to Philippi or an amalgam of possibly several letters.

When was it written?

Our estimate of the date when Philippians was written is determined by our view of where Paul was when he wrote the letter. Our main clue is that Paul wrote Philippians from prison and we know that he suffered at least two major spells there.

Acts 16 tells us that Paul arrived at Philippi during what we now refer to as his second missionary journey, probably around AD 48 or 49. A church was soon formed but, following trouble roused by hostility to Paul's healing work, Paul and his companions were forced to leave. In 1 Thessalonians 2, verse 2, Paul refers to 'all the injury and outrage which as you know we had suffered at Philippi. . .'

He had no further contact with the infant congregation there, apart from the gifts of money they sent him in Thessalonica and also later in Corinth, until he sent Timothy to Macedonia and then later passed through Macedonia himself twice. Some time later, prevented from returning to Philippi by an imprisonment, Paul wrote to the congregation there.[2]

We know from Acts that Paul was imprisoned at Caesarea around AD 56 and, later, at Rome in about AD 58 to 60.[3] Either of these imprisonments could have been the occasion of his writing to the Philippians; arguments may be advanced for and against each alternative.

From internal evidence provided by the letter to the Philippians, we can see that there was considerable traffic of people and news between Paul and the congregation, and an imprisonment at Caesarea would allow for this. The Philippians heard of Paul's imprisonment and sent Epaphroditus to assist him. Epaphroditus fell ill and news of this reached the church at Philippi, causing them anxiety which was then reported to Paul.

When Epaphroditus had recovered, Paul sent him to Philippi, expressing the hope that he could send Timothy soon in advance of a visit which he hoped himself to make on his release from prison.[4] This suggests an imprisonment relatively close to Philippi to allow for all this coming and going and, on that basis, Caesarea would be the more likely choice as the place of writing.

However, against this, the situation mentioned in chapter 1, verse 15 onwards could well be thought to favour Rome. Paul has already faced a hearing — could it have been in Rome? — which has established that his 'crime' is Christianity.[5] Paul also enjoys a certain amount of freedom to associate with colleagues such as Timothy and Epaphroditus. This could well be thought to comply with the circumstances described in Acts 28, verses 30 and 31 — well after his arrival in Rome. Finally, there are preachers in the community where Paul is imprisoned, who hold different theological views about Paul — and express them in their preaching! — and this would appear more likely in a large city such as Rome, where Paul had been personally unknown prior to his arrival under arrest.

However, Paul's long-cherished hope to leave Rome and travel to Spain would have taken him in the opposite direction from Philippi and his letter to the Philippians does express the hope that he will be able to revisit his friends at Philippi on release.[6] On balance, I prefer the Caesarean alternative, although there is nothing to offer conclusive proof about this. Caesarea would imply, therefore, a date of writing around AD 58.

One letter or three?

The question about the integrity of the letter mainly concerns the abrupt transition in atmosphere at the beginning of chapter 3. The first verse begins either with a wish that the Philippians experience the joy of the Lord or, in fact, a farewell leave-taking. The Greek word that is used, *chairete*, may be translated 'rejoice' or 'farewell'. Immediately afterwards there is the very polemical outburst against the advocates of circumcision.

This disjointedness of thought has led to various theories that the letter as we now have it is an amalgam of two or possibly three separate letters. Some have even thought that the wording of the second part of verse 1 of chapter 3, 'to repeat what I have written to you before. . .', implies a previous correspondence with the Philippians.

Readers with a taste for this kind of detective work are referred to the more technical commentaries for a full discussion. The French scholar J.F. Collange argues for our letter being a compilation of three different letters, while the theologians R.P. Martin and Gerald Hawthorne argue for the integrity of the letter as we have it.

An overview

It is valuable for us to remember that when Paul wrote this letter he was in prison, uncertain of the outcome of his trial, but realising that he faced the possibility of being sentenced to death. He writes to friends who have supported him in his work and he shares with them the range of feelings which his circumstances produce in his mind. The letter he writes is one of the warmest, richest and most joyful documents in the New Testament!

As we read this letter, we cannot fail to be impressed by the vitality of Paul's faith, the range of issues in his own life and in the lives of his correspondents which his faith lights up, and the sheer confidence in Jesus Christ which informs what he says. It can be summed up, and the key to the means of fulfilment in Paul's view can be discerned, in these words of chapter 1, verse 21: 'For me, life is Christ. . .'

Paul's testimony, given in all the personal detail of this letter, is that Jesus Christ and faith in him provide the meaning to life and the means of fulfilment.

Christ offers fulfilment by affirming Paul as a person: chapter 3 makes clear that his career and ambitions are set on a more solid foundation by Christ. Christ offers fulfilment by inspiring Paul to cope with adversity and hardship: his strength is supplied by Christ.[7]

Paul's knowledge of how we are to live — in unity within the fellowship of the church, in love and support of one another, and in humility before God and in obedience to his way[8] — is in every case rooted and grounded in the love God has revealed toward us in Christ.

Biblical scholar F.W. Beare sees the central ethical issues in the book as 'to live worthily of Christ's gospel, to be committed in mind and spirit, to be considerate and humble, to trust God and to make our requests known to him in prayer, and to keep our minds fixed on all that is true or noble and commendable.'[9]

It is worth noting that, in the incidental details of the letter, Paul also shows that others, too, had found in Christ the fulfilment of their lives — Timothy, Epaphroditus and all the others whom he names as he writes. They shared in the fulfilment which trust in Christ had brought. Their experience offers an incentive and an invitation to the modern reader to share in it, too.

Viktor Frankl summed up what he had learned in the concentration camps of World War II by saying: 'He who knows the *why* for his existence will be able to bear almost any *how*.'[10]

Paul had found his 'why' in Jesus Christ and the significance of that relationship filled his life. There is ample confirmation in this letter that he had found his fulfilment in Christ as well.

Discussion questions

Talking it through

1 When people write a letter, what are they usually trying to do? What is Paul trying to do in this letter?

2 From what you have already been told in the *Introduction*, what key events surround this letter? How does this help us understand Philippians?

3 Paul writes this letter from prison. Do you think this influenced his writing? How? (After you have finished reading Philippians, come back to your conclusions here and see if your response has changed.)

4 People are preoccupied with 'being fulfilled'. What, for Paul, is the source of true fulfilment? What is the key difference between his attitude and our attitude today?

 **Widening our horizons**

1 Letter-writing is a lost art. Does letter-writing have a place today as a means of practical encouragement? Give an example.

2 Experience is a great teacher. What recent experience have you had which proved a surprising teacher?

3 Which of the following gives you the greatest sense of fulfilment and why:
  (a) your career
  (b) others' respect for you
  (c) your physical and emotional well-being
  (d) your family?

4 What light does knowing the 'why' for your existence throw on the following life situations:
  (a) wrongful conviction that results in your imprisonment
  (b) contracting AIDS from a blood transfusion
  (c) unexpectedly inheriting enough money to live off your investments
  (d) the death of your only rival for the job you have always wanted?

1
The prayer of faith

What difference does faith make?
PHILIPPIANS 1, VERSES 1 TO 11

WHAT DOES IT MEAN to be a Christian, to be 'a person of faith'? One of the best answers to that question was given by the apostle Paul when he wrote to the church at Corinth: 'So if anyone is in Christ, there is a new creation: everything old has passed away; see, everything has become new!' (2 Corinthians 5, verse 17).

In other words, when a person shares their life with Jesus Christ, everything starts afresh: there is a new beginning. Christ moves in and nothing remains the same.

The new beginning (verses 1 to 7)
Paul himself is an example of the new beginning

which Christ produces. In this letter he gives evidence that Jesus Christ is in control. Any contemporary of Paul's writing to the Philippians would have begun, 'Gaius, to the Philippians: Greetings.' Paul takes a quite different tack in verses 1 and 2; the difference is caused by Jesus Christ:

> Paul and Timothy, servants of Christ Jesus. To all the saints in Christ Jesus who are in Philippi, with the bishops and deacons: Grace to you and peace from God our Father and the Lord Jesus Christ.

Three times Jesus Christ is mentioned — he has impinged even on the way Paul writes his letters! And this happens, because Jesus has impinged on the lives of Paul and the people to whom he writes.

❐ *The new community*
One of the marks of the new beginning Christ makes possible is the creation of a new community. Paul was instrumental in the creation of the church at Philippi. As a result of his preaching of the gospel — the story is told in Acts 16, verses 11 to 40 — people who were very different from one another had found in his preaching the message they were needing. They accepted Paul's preaching of Jesus Christ, put their faith in Christ and then became an infant church at Philippi — a new community of Christian love, support and encouragement.

Paul and many of the Christians in the early church carried that sense of community with them — and derived strength and encouragement from the support which being in Christ's new community brought. Verses 4 to 7 here is a good example. Paul writes from prison, fully aware that he might lose his case and be put to death, but he is nonetheless full of faith and joy. What he means in these four verses is that, when people become Christians, they are linked to a new community — to people of love, encouragement and concern, who share their faith and who want to share it with other people in the world.

But we must be careful: it would be easy to stress the communal aspects of the Christian faith and neglect the *personal* aspects, to generalise and neglect the implications for our individual lives. That's a perpetual temptation in many walks of life, including the Christian one.

There's a story from a mining village in Scotland. Friction had arisen when a politically committed youngster joined the colliery team. He was always badgering his work-mates about the benefits of communism. One member of the team decided to sort him out.

'So communism means that if you had two houses, you would give me one?'

'Sure.'

'And if you had two cars, you would give me one?

'Sure.'

'And if you had two greyhounds, you'd give me one?'

'Steady on, mate,' came the reply. 'I've already got two greyhounds!'

It's always easy to talk generalities and leave oneself out of consideration — to talk about the Christian faith and not about *my* Christian faith. To do that is to get the balance wrong. Part of the new beginning of faith is the new person which Christ makes possible.

❏ *The new person*

Paul also provides a good example for us here. We will read his own account in chapter 3, verses 4 to 14 of the changes Christ brought to his life. In that passage he describes all the important aspects of his life which become 'garbage' after he put Jesus Christ in charge of his life.

One small indication of this same process may be seen in his opening comments in the letter. He begins, 'Paul and Timothy, servants of Jesus Christ' (verse 1). Now in terms of experience there's no doubt who was the senior and who was the junior colleague in that partnership. But precedence is of no significance: in Christ they are equal and in Christ's service equally important. It is highly likely that Paul includes Timothy like this in the opening address of the letter because he seeks to encourage and build up Timothy in his work for Jesus.

I don't think it matters whether you describe Paul's servanthood role as a new love, a new humility or a new zeal to see the kingdom of God advance. It is, in fact, all of these — and more. Paul in Christ is a different person and his main priority now is to advance Christ's kingdom. Whoever is the catalyst — he, Timothy, or any of the people of Philippi — is really of no consequence.

When Christian faith is healthy, that's how it is. We lose self-centred ambitions and concerns, and they are replaced by concerns for Christ and the extension of his kingdom. I love the way German theologian Karl Barth exemplified this characteristic on one occasion. He was a prodigious writer with worldwide influence, and his work has been honoured and acclaimed in many ways.

Towards the end of his life an 81-year-old lady wrote to him, thanking him for a book of his sermons which she read to her 98-year-old friend in the nursing home where they were living — they were both too frail to attend church. Barth replied:

Dear Mrs Heim,
I have no fewer than eleven honorary doctorates, but consider this. None has given me more pleasure than your little letter in which you told me that my books affect you and your even older friend so much and are so understandable and so useful in your lives. . .[11]

His primary interest was sharing the Christian faith and helping people develop that faith. And to help us in this, Christ offers new resources.[11]

☐ *The new resources*
Paul writes: 'Grace to you and peace, from God our Father and the Lord Jesus Christ' (verse 2). That verse contains the reference to the new resources — God's grace and God's peace.

'Grace' is one of the key words in the New Testament. It means undeserved favour or uncalculating love. It is the supreme characteristic by which Jesus Christ lived: he was 'full of grace and truth' (John 1, verse 14). In Paul's letters, God's grace is the goodness which seeks and claims us in Christ and which loves us even when we are utterly unlovable.

Paul's autobiography in the passage we've referred to (in chapter 3) shows this clearly. There, he says, he persecuted the church — but God forgave him and accepted him. That's God's grace at work in his life.

Fred Craddock makes this perceptive comment about grace: 'Given the sinful conditions that determine our granting or withholding a blessing, for any of us to desire God's unmerited favour upon other persons is certainly due to the presence in us of a God who sends sun and rain upon good and evil alike (Matthew 5, verse 45) and who is kind even to the grateful and selfish (Luke 6, verse 35).'[12]

God's peace is the assurance that those whom God loves he will never forsake. Paul is in prison as he writes this letter and he half-expects the imprisonment to lead to his death — but he's not unduly concerned. His confidence that he can let God 'order and provide' is expressed unforgettably in chapter 4, verse 7: 'And the peace of God, which passes all understanding, shall guard your hearts and minds in Jesus Christ our Lord.'

Grace is where God loves me and makes me his own, even though I have done nothing to deserve it. *Peace* is where I am convinced that all this true. These are the resources of faith.

Thus the opening to this letter shows us the new beginning Christ offers. It helps us to see some of the benefits Jesus Christ brings when we put him in charge of our lives. That's part of what it means to be a Christian.

Paul's prayer (verses 8 to 11)

Nothing reveals the quality of the new relationships which are possible within the Christian community better than the prayer which Paul offers for his friends at Philippi. Of all the letters to churches which Paul wrote that have survived in our New Testament — Colossians 4, verse 16 indicates there were others — the letter to the church at Philippi is the warmest and most affectionate. It shows the extent to which Christian love can and should bind together brothers and sisters of faith.

This love is marked by the joy and delight of sharing one another's company. Paul longs to be with his friends once again. In verse 8, he says that he longs for these people as deeply as Jesus himself does. Part of that longing for the Philippians is the longing to see them grow and develop in their faith, so that he can help them 'determine what is best' (verse 10). As already mentioned, chapter 3 of this letter records Paul's experience of discovering what is best in life, what really matters. And what is that?

One theologian described religion as the state of 'being grasped by an ultimate concern'. What he meant was that, while our lives are filled with many concerns — some of them necessary, some of them important, some of them trivial — there is one concern which dwarfs all others, one concern which is utterly fundamental to our lives. Now whatever that ultimate concern is, *that* is one's religion.

Thus for one person, her ultimate concern may be her career; for another it may be making money; for a third it may be sport or leisure pursuits. Whatever it is, that concern functions in the individual's life as a religion: it is the thing that matters above all else.

Paul could say: 'I want to know Christ and the power of his resurrection' (chapter 3, verse 10). He was in no doubt that that was what ultimately concerned him. And it was for a similar ultimate concern on the part of his beloved Philippians that he prayed.

Philippians 3 makes it clear that this knowledge of Christ puts us right with God and gives us what Paul calls the righteousness that 'comes through faith in Christ' as we become like him in his death' (chapter 3, verses 9 and 10). The end result of a life thus lived in dependence on and in obedience to Jesus Christ will be that we can stand before Christ on Judgement Day 'pure and blameless' (chapter 1, verse 10) – put right with God through our faith in his Son, Jesus Christ.

Paul thus makes it clear that the faith which begins as God's *gift to us* in Christ ends as God's *achievement in us* through Christ, so that he alone deserves the credit. This is the truth which Paul expresses in these memorable words from Ephesians 2, verses 8 to 10:

> For by grace you have been saved through faith, and this is not your own doing; it is the gift of God — not the result of works, so that no-one may boast. For we are what he has made us, created in Christ Jesus for good works, which God prepared beforehand to be our way of life.

As Fred Craddock says, being blameless leaves 'no room for pride or superior holiness. No reason to be keeping score, for such lives are the fulfilment of that gift of righteousness which comes from God.'[13]

Discussion questions

Talking it through

1 What types of sharing are mentioned in verses 3 to 7?

How does this sharing work? Why is it the essence of Christian community?

2 Paul describes himself as a servant. What evidence is there in verses 1 to 7 to show what a true servant is like?

Put in your own words what you think is, in essence, the attitude of the true servant.

3 What picture of God does the term 'grace' conjure up? Why might people sometimes be uncomfortable with this concept of God?

4 From Paul's prayer in verses 10 and 11, what do we learn is his ambition for his Philippian friends? How does he hope they will fulfil this expectation?

The prayer of faith/31

 **Widening our horizons**

1 Look at Paul's words in verses 4 to 7. Does he evidence a healthy dependence on others, or an unhealthy co-dependence — a compulsive reliance on others?

What are examples of good dependence in each of the following relationships:
(a) the relationship between husband and wife?
(b) the relationship between parents and their adult children?
(c) the relationship between members of a mature church?

2 Take these imaginary situations and suggest what it might mean to 'show grace' in each case:
(a) a politician of one party towards a politician from an opposing party
(b) a motorist towards a woman whose car has broken down on a lonely stretch of road at midnight
(c) a murderer who asks a surviving family member forgiveness after having killed all the other members of the family.

Can grace be just too hard for us, a quality that only God can show?

3 Rank each of the following types of peace in order of importance for you and explain why you have ranked them so:
(a) international peace
(b) peace with our neighbours next door
(c) peace with our spouse/children/parents
(d) a sense of acceptance of ourselves as we are
(e) peace with God
Is there a connection between the different types of peace?

4 What is your ultimate concern in life? Look at each of the following questions, answering them as honestly as possible.
(a) What work would you most like to do if you had a choice?
(b) What do you like to spend your money on?
(c) What do you *most* want for your children/parents/spouse?
(d) What prayer do you *most* want answered?
Are there any other conclusions you can draw from your answers?

2
The courage of faith

Can faith survive when up against it?
PHILIPPIANS CHAPTER 1, VERSES 12 TO 30

THESE VERSES RAISE ISSUES that you will encounter any day in the headlines of the world's press. In a sense, they unite the 'long ago' of scripture with the 'now' of daily living. They deal with oppression, imprisonment, torture and the risk of death in the same way as do many news stories coming out of places of oppression and conflict today.

Many Christians in the twentieth century fight conditions which others have never been called upon to face. Through their struggle, they have discovered something of the power of the Christian faith even under the most hostile of conditions. Their experience matches Paul's: one can make great discoveries about the Christian faith under oppression, even in prison.

Think of the situation facing Christians in China, for example, who are denied access to university education or worthwhile careers because of their faith. Before 1989 conditions were similar in East Germany, and yet the East German church remained vigorous and faithful under pressure and was instrumental in bringing about the unprecedented changes which the world has witnessed in that country — without violence. In China, too, there has been a faithful church working quietly under difficult conditions.

Far too many people around the world still face oppression, imprisonment, torture and death. But the experience of people of faith is that these difficulties do not have the final word.

Many Christians who are caught up in situations of oppression willingly view their predicament as a struggle for faith — for the dignity of humankind and for the quality of human life. Their courage and faithfulness encourage us and the lessons they learn enrich us.

This truth was given unforgettable expression in the words of a prayer found beside the emaciated body of a little boy at the Ravensbruck concentration camp in 1945. The prayer reads:

> O Lord, remember not only the men and women of goodwill, but also those of ill-will. Do not remember all the suffering they have inflicted on

us; remember the fruits we have brought, thanks
to that suffering — our comradeship, our loyalty,
our humility, our courage, our generosity, the
greatness of heart which has grown out of all
this. . .[14]

They achieved these positive results, they learned
these lessons — even in the concentration camps!
You can make a discovery about faith — even in
prison!

Paul did. We don't exactly know all the details
of the imprisonment he was undergoing when he
wrote his letter to the Philippians, but his discovery
so filled him with faith and confidence that his letter
is among the most positive things he ever wrote,
pulsating with faith, hope and love.

In his writings from prison, Paul is able to claim
that he shared a great faith and that he worshipped
a great God. This is an important truth — one that's
worth bringing from the long ago of the Bible into
the now of today. Let's look at both these aspects:

❐ *Paul is able to claim he shares a great faith*
You'd think Paul would have been depressed in
prison, but he was not — he was filled with faith.
You'd think he would have been worried about the
progress of the mission with its most energetic missionary locked away. He was not. Rather, as he
says in verse 13, he was full of wonder as he realised
that the gospel was advancing into sections of society

which it might otherwise never have penetrated. Paul realised with joy that God was at work, the gospel was spreading and the faith was advancing — even without him!

What happened was that during a long-drawn-out imprisonment, many Roman officers and soldiers involved in his case heard about it, perhaps because they were on duty while he defended himself, or they may possibly have spoken to him in prison or on the way to and from court. And, if this was during his Caesarean imprisonment, two Roman governors and King Herod Agrippa and their wives heard him — and one of these governors used to send for him frequently to talk about his faith.

The result of this was that all the interest in Christianity which his case generated gave new advantages to local Christians where Paul was imprisoned (verse 14). Christianity became hot news. They were able to witness and make new converts — and the church began growing as a result.

And even if some who disagreed with Paul used the occasion to preach with the unworthy motive of somehow making things more difficult for Paul and adding to his burdens, the result of that merely led to more people hearing the gospel. Thus the message spread even more widely!

☐ *Paul is able to claim he worships a great God*
The greatness of God is seen, not just in the fact he advanced the gospel through 'earthen vessels' like

Paul, or that he spread the faith even through the preaching of those whose motives were unworthy, self-centred and cruel. Even more, his greatness is seen in the way he worked on Paul.

Paul had been treated badly — as we read in verses 15 to 17. We don't know how his opponents thought they could harass him by their preaching — that's one detail of the story we can't figure out. But they did hope to make his case harder to win and they may even have hoped (as some commentators suggest) to make sure he was given the death penalty.

Now Paul was hurt by their actions. He was angry at them — with good cause. So he exposed their motives to the light of truth — he talked about their 'envy and rivalry' (verse 15) and their 'selfish ambition' (verse 17), acknowledging the distress they had caused him. Notice, however, what he said in verse 18: 'What does it matter? Just this, that Christ is proclaimed in every way, whether out of false motives or true; and in that I rejoice.'

Fred Craddock points out that there is an important principle at work here: 'The power of the gospel is not contingent upon the motives and feelings of the one preaching. . . too much introspection can immobilise the church. . . too many. . . have been made to feel guilty because on a given day they laboured from commitment rather than a warm heart.'[15]

But what is most noteworthy is that God had taken away Paul's bitterness and replaced it with trust and faith; God has healed him from the injury which they had inflicted upon him. Here lies the real greatness of God.

Paul told his friends these details because he wanted them to believe, whatever their adversity, in a great God and affirm the transforming power of the Christian faith. He wanted them to understand that, when they prayed, they could know that they were praying to a God who is powerfully active in human life, capable of bringing good out of evil.

That is an important discovery to bring from the long ago of scripture into the now of our lives today. It's a discovery which men and women of faith have also made in the twentieth century.

For example, take this detail from the life of Oscar Romero, who served for many years as the Roman Catholic Archbishop of El Salvador. Just before he was assassinated in 1980, he telephoned a message to the Mexican newspaper *Excelsior*, in which he said:

> I have often been threatened with death. Nevertheless, as a Christian, I do not believe in death without resurrection... You may say, if they succeed in killing me, that I pardon and bless the people who do the deed. Would that they might be convinced they are wasting their time!
> A bishop will die, but the church of God...
> will never perish.

Here there is an awareness of the greatness of the faith and the greatness of God. It is deeply moving to see that Romero has no more bitterness in his heart than Paul did in his.

There are many places in the world today where people are oppressed and imprisoned, tortured and killed, often for their faith, often for their stand — inspired by faith — for human rights.

If, like the church at Philippi, we learn to align ourselves with suffering brothers and sisters around the world, share indirectly in their struggle and uphold them in their need with our prayers, I believe we can help advance their cause and make the same great discovery: we share a great faith and we worship a great God.

Foundations of faith (verses 18 to 26)

A crisis can bring the best out in a person: the pressure of the moment reveals qualities and strengths which were always present, but which may not have been seen until the crisis brought them out.

These verses allow us a very impressive glimpse of the apostle Paul under pressure and reveal the strength of his life. To all outward appearances, Paul is up against it. He is imprisoned for his faith, uncertain whether the outcome of his trial will be life or death, separated from his friends and harassed by some vindictive opponents. He is deeply uncertain about what lies ahead. Despite all that, he speaks — twice! — of joy, and he radiates assurance and faith in all he writes.

How does he do it? I think Paul would answer such a question by saying, 'I don't. Christ does it for me.' As he will tell his friends at the end of this letter, 'I can do all things through him who gives me strength.' In the heat of the crisis, Paul lets us see that the basis for his confidence and courage — indeed, the basis of all his living — was his relationship with Jesus Christ. This is most clearly expressed in verse 21, 'For to me, living is Christ and dying is gain.' These verses bring out the significance of that thought.

☐ *Jesus gives strength through prayer (verses 18 to 21)*
Jesus is the source of Paul's strength, and one way of receiving this strength is through prayer, a point he makes in verses 18 and 19.

Christians know why this is so. Prayer takes us (and those we pray for) closer into the presence of God, into the sphere of his love, into the realm of the Spirit where God is at work for good for those who love him. Paul has expressed this thought in Romans 8, verses 26 to 28:

> The Spirit helps us in our weakness; for we do not know how to pray as we ought, but that very Spirit intercedes with sighs too deep for words. . . the Spirit intercedes for the saints according to the will of God. We know that all things work together for good for those who love God, who are called according to his purpose.

When we pray and are prayed for, we are offered strength from Jesus Christ. Many Christians have been able to confirm this in their own experience. One confirmation comes from a time when believers in what was then the Soviet Union were being persecuted for their faith.

The speaker is Anatoli Levitin, who was imprisoned and put in solitary confinement in the 1970s for giving religious instruction to young people. His solitary confinement turned out to be a blessing in disguise — he was able to pray undisturbed! He wrote:

> The greatest miracle of all is prayer. I have only to turn my thoughts to God and I suddenly feel a force bursting into me; there is new strength in my soul, in my entire being . . . Not only my own prayer helped me, but even more the prayer of many other faithful Christians. I felt it continually, working from a distance, lifting me up as though on wings, giving me living water and the bread of life, peace of soul, rest and love.[16]

That is an exact parallel to the experience Paul is describing here. The assurance he receives is indicated in verse 20: 'It is my eager expectation and hope that I will not be put to shame in any way, but that by my speaking with all boldness, Christ will be exalted now as always in my body whether by life or by death.' He knows that Jesus answers prayer!

I would like to think that contemporary Christians might be encouraged and inspired by these verses. All those who sometimes struggle in their prayer life should find reassurance in the thought that the Spirit intercedes for us. Those who are members of a church might reflect on how often and how seriously they pray for their churches and Christian leaders. And they might draw encouragement from the power of prayer to which Paul bears witness, and make connection with Jesus' prayer for his disciples: 'Simon, Simon, listen! Satan has demanded to sift all of you like wheat, but I have prayed for you that your faith may not fail' (Luke 22, verse 31). Fred Craddock makes the implications of this clear:

> Christian leaders are not those exempt from fear, doubt, discouragement and repeated testing but those who are supported by prayer and who, through repentence and forgiveness, find grace and strength to continue.[17]

❑ *Jesus is at the centre (verse 22)*
Paul's relationship with Jesus Christ is also seen in the place Jesus occupies in Paul's life including, of course, his church life. This emerges at two points in this passage. The first is in verse 22, where Paul says, 'If I am to live in the flesh, that means fruitful labour for me. . .' He does not define what the labour is, but it is clear that Paul is speaking of his

missionary labour here, the work of extending the kingdom, to which he gave himself wholeheartedly.

This is frequently Paul's meaning when he uses the word 'labour', as examples such as Romans 15, verse 18, 2 Corinthians 10, verse 11, and Philippians 2, verse 30 bear out. A parallel usage is the way he often speaks of 'fellow-workers' when he means, in fact, other missionaries (see, for example, Philippians 2, verse 25, Philippians 4, verse 3 and Romans 16, verses 3, 9 and 21). In Paul's letters, 'labour' or 'work' was almost a shorthand way of describing his church work. This work was often conducted on a full-time basis (to use the modern expression). But 'work' could also be applied to the church work of members of congregations who were not full-time church workers.

At the end of 1 Corinthians 15, Paul offers encouragement to all the Christians at Corinth by saying in verse 58, 'Therefore, my beloved, be steadfast, immovable, always excelling in the work of the Lord, because you know that in the Lord your labour is not in vain.' It is Christ's work which the believer seeks to carry out and (even when sometimes motives may be awry, as we saw above in verses 15 to 18) Christ will bless it. As long as the believer remains 'in Christ', her service will be fruitful (see John 15, verse 5).

But Jesus is also the focus of the life of the whole church: in verse 27 Paul hopes, when released, to meet up again with his friends at Philippi 'so that I may share abundantly in your boasting in Christ Jesus'. There is a little uncertainty about Paul's meaning, but the translation given here (from the NRSV) seems the most likely sense of Paul's words.

Paul writes frequently about boasting in his letters, in all the shades of meaning which the word carries in our usage today. There are references to the kind of boasting that is self-advertisement (see, for example, Romans 3, verse 27 and Ephesians 2, verse 9). There are references to the kind of boasting that is virtually a form of self-defence in response to personal criticism such as Paul was reluctantly driven to in 2 Corinthians 10 to 13 (see, for example chapter 12, verses 1, 5 and 6). However, the type of boasting he has in view in verse 27 is the boasting which is a celebration of what God has done in Christ. Paul virtually defines Christians in Romans 5, verse 11 as those who 'boast in God through our Lord Jesus Christ, through whom we have now received reconciliation'. Twice in his letters to Corinth he alludes to Jeremiah 9, verses 23 and 24: 'Let the one who boasts, boast in the Lord' (1 Corinthians 1, verse 31 and 2 Corinthains 10, verse 17).

What Paul is saying is that whenever he and the Philippians meet again, it will be to share together in celebrating the great things Jesus Christ has done. Of course, most immediately they will be celebrating Paul's deliverance (see verse 19). This gives us an informative glimpse into what was central in the relationship between Paul and the Philippians. Their fellowship with one another was strong and deep, but their fellowship in celebration of Christ was stronger. Jesus is the centre, Jesus is the cause, Jesus is the point of all their fellowship within the church.

It is often easy to blur the central focus of church life. We can be busy with preoccupations which, if we are not careful, may virtually exclude Jesus Christ or relegate him to a minor position. A business agenda within the church may be so time-consuming as to leave little or no time for celebrating the great things God has done. As a result, prayer, Bible study and the testimony of personal experience of God's grace become minority activities. In consequence, we are often under-nourished and over-stretched in our Christian life and feel that encouragements are few and far between.

In his book *On Being A Christian*, Hans Kung complains about the way the word 'Christian' has been devalued — worn bare by over-use and inappropriate use. He proposes a clear remedy: 'The Christianity of the Christians must remain Christian. But it remains Christian only if it remains expressly committed to the one Christ.' Paul's concentration on the centrality of Christ in this passage should bring us back to basics: Jesus Christ at the centre of all our church life.[18]

☐ Jesus is the hope for the future (verse 23)

Paul has not lost sight of the possibility that his trial might not result in his deliverance — despite what he writes in verse 19. He does not, however, worry about death — he knows it will take him nearer the Lord. Behind this statement are Jesus' words that those who believe in him have (here and now) eternal life; it begins now, and it continues through and beyond death.

Paul is not specific about what the afterlife may be like in this verse. In other places — 1 Thessalonians 4, verses 13 to 18 and 1 Corinthians 15 — he addressed questions about death and resurrection. Here he does not reflect on where heaven is located; how (or when) it is reached; or who will be there. For him it is enough that he will be with Jesus and that such a life will be 'far better' than anything experienced thus far. In the face of the prospect of death, nothing else matters than the knowledge that Jesus, whose love we have experienced in this life, is greater than anything else, and is able to hold us in time and in eternity.

The hope which Paul here expresses in Christ the Lord of life and death has brought comfort and strength to many Christians as they have faced the prospect of their own death. When John A. T. Robinson knew he was dying, he preached a sermon on death in the chapel of Trinity College, Cambridge. Incidentally, part of the sermon demonstrates the way in which a knowledge of the teaching of scripture may bring help in time of need. Robinson wove together several passages from Paul's letters — Romans 5, verses 1 to 5 and 2 Corinthians 4, verses 10 to 12 — before taking up Philippians 1, verses 23 to 24. He said:

> The Christian takes his stand not on optimism but on hope. This is based not on rosy prognosis (from the human point of view mine is bleak) but, as St Paul says, on suffering. For this, he says, trains us to endure, and endurance brings proof that we have stood the test, and this proof is the ground of hope — in the God who can bring resurrection out and through the other side of death. That is why he also says that, though we carry death with us in our bodies (all of us), we never cease to be confident.
>
> His prayer is that 'always the greatness of Christ will shine out clearly in my person, whether through my life or through my death. For to me life is Christ and death gain; but what if my living on in the body may serve some good purpose? Which then am I to choose? I cannot tell. I am torn two ways: what I should like' — he says more confidently than most of us could — 'is to depart and be with Christ, that is better by far; but for your sake there is greater need for me to stay on in the body.'
>
> According to my chronology he lived nearly ten years after writing those words: others would say it was shorter. But how little does it

matter. He had passed beyond time and its calculations. He had risen with Christ.[19]

In these words Robinson illustrates what should always be central in our handling of scripture. The truths of scripture bear testimony to Christ and his eternal love for his children. They are given to offer comfort and support in our times of difficulty, danger or death. That had been Paul's purpose in writing to his friends at Philippi, and the eternal truths he affirmed live on in Christian faith to help believers of every generation.

Encouragement and support (verses 27 to 30)

We are all aware of the phenomenon of the modern city. As cities grow in size, they become more impersonal and anonymous. The bigger they become, the easier it is for crime to gain a hold and for social problems to increase. When this happens, people grab hold of any scheme which encourages community involvement and support.

Two of the best known of these are the Safety House scheme and Neighbourhood Watch. In many communities a number of private homes have been designated 'Safety Houses' to offer shelter to children who may at times feel at risk on the streets. Children know that if they feel afraid, a Safety House will offer safety and shelter. Neighbourhood Watch encourages us all to keep a protective eye on our neighbour's property and report anything suspicious to the proper authorities.

What is happening in these ventures, of course, is that ordinary people are pooling their resources and finding opportunities to assist one another. They are regaining some control of their lives and exercising some responsiblity for their own personal well-being. The basic presupposition to such schemes is that, in any community, we belong to one another and can help and support our fellow citizens.

That is a very Christian concept. It expresses a part of what it means for us to belong to Jesus Christ and his church, and it explains what, as Christians, we may give to and receive from one another.

Paul touches on aspects of this in this section from chapter 1. He gives his readers advice in Christian living and, as he does so, he touches on aspects of community support which the church can provide its members. In these verses, he affirms the basic truth that the Christian church is also a community within which we belong to one another, and where we can help and support each other.

In verse 27 he says, 'Live your life in a manner worthy of the gospel of Christ' and, to enable the Philippians to act on his instruction, he reveals the church to be a community of encouragement. In Paul's view, as expressed in these verses, the Christian is not left alone to struggle with the task of witnessing to her faith. As well as the strength which God supplies, there is support and encouragement to be derived from fellow-believers. Paul suggests in verses 27 and 28 that being a Christian involves a struggle with opposition, in which the believer requires strength and support from both God and others.

The Philippian Christians knew the reality of opposition at first hand. According to Acts 16, verses 16 to 24, Paul had confronted a slave girl during his mission to Philippi. The girl had made money for her owners by telling fortunes and, when Paul healed her, they disguised their resentment at the loss of their income by starting a commotion, purportedly on religious grounds. This was calculated to enlist support by tapping into people's insecurities about religious or cultural innovations, and that insecurity was rife in Paul's day.

The culture of the first century Roman empire was suffering from what Gilbert Murray called 'the failure of nerve'. The old landmarks had gone, and with them the old values and standards. Many people turned to eastern religions, mystery cults and astrology to try to find meaning and inner security. It was an era of spiritual confusion, anxiety and loss of confidence, and in some ways it was not very different to what many people today are experiencing.

Contemporary society operates under similar pressures: industry, business, politics, education all seem to be infected with some such downward pull. A cynic might be tempted to observe that often the least that we can get away with is the most that we will offer.

But the high ground *is* there. For example, Professor David Pennington of Melbourne has said: 'Education is about achieving the greatest potential for each individual.' It's not just education that should be about achieving the greatest potential for each individual — it should be every aspect of our life: our politics, our industry and commerce, our law, our medicine.

The Christian faith affirms the unique importance of each one of us; it declares that God loves us enough to have given his Son to die for us. It lives on the strength of what ordinary people like ourselves have done in response to the transforming power of the gospel as it was experienced, for instance, by Peter or Paul and all the others who, according to Acts 17, verse 6, turned 'the world upside down' in Jesus' name.

This is what Paul had in mind when he wrote in verse 27 that the Philippians should 'live in a manner worthy of the gospel'. The Christian faith affirms the value of each individual and offers the believers the incentive to release that potential into the life and service of the Christian community as a whole (see 1 Corinthians, verse 12). Paul sought to encourage the Philippians to work together towards that end — 'standing firm in one spirit, striving side by side with one mind' (verse 27). To live worthily of the gospel means that Christians should be asking, 'What can I do? Where can I be of service? How can I contribute to the common task?' and should be finding through the support of the church community opportunities to translate such questions into actions.

The privilege of belief and suffering (verses 29 and 30)

There is much in the world which does not want to accept the transformation God offers. Paul acknowledges as much when he says that we share the privilege of suffering for him. The Philippians would know exactly what he meant. We read in Acts 16 that Paul was attacked and imprisoned because he helped and healed a poor demented slave girl. The people who were deriving a living from her affliction were furious with Paul and stirred up trouble for him. These people put profit before people and did not care who was hurt, so long as the money flowed in.

Is it any different today? People today profit from drugs, gambling, prostitution and other such vices. In a society which tolerates abuses like that, Christians who affirm their faith and stand up for the values Christianity embraces will soon find themselves unpopular and swimming uncomfortably against the tide.

But Paul's experience would be that there are compensations. His ordeal in Philippi became a vibrant testimony to his faith and, according to Acts chapter 16, led directly to the conversion at least of the jailer and his family.

Many Christians today could attest that their experience has been similar to the apostle's. For example, Dr David Read of New York was invited some years ago to conduct a student mission in Adelaide. The Immaterialist Society of the university who were mostly agnostics and atheists campaigned widely and publicly to discredit the mission. At his opening address, the front rows of the hall were full of agnostic opponents. After he finished speaking, time was allowed for questions and debate and the arguments raged for several hours. In his autobiography, Read writes:

> It was the best frank exchange of views on religion I have ever taken part in — so good, in fact, that the following afternoon I offered the floor to the president of the agnostic group and we had another ding-dong theological battle. From then on the mission was the main event on the campus. . .

Many people, some years later, spoke of the positive impact which that mission had had on their lives. Read concluded: 'It goes to show what the presence of live opposition can do for the proclamation of the gospel.'[20]

Simply to read that testimony is to be encouraged by the writer's experience of the power of the gospel to confront and challenge hostile and opposing viewpoints.

In the Christian faith we encounter a God who gives his people strength and support through the Bible, prayer, worship and sacrament, and through other believers. It is important for believers to tap into these strengths.

Discussion questions

Talking it through

1 What two unexpected benefits did Paul's imprisonment actually bring? See verses 12 to 14.
   Is it possible to generalise and say that persecution is always a good thing? Why/why not?

2 Paul had a very relaxed attitude to his own importance as a preacher of the gospel (verses 15 to 18). Do today's preachers take themselves too seriously? What makes Paul's approach so refreshing?

3 Paul seemed almost to have a death wish (verses 23 and 24) — or does he? See verses 25 and 26.

4 Think about Paul's concept of living 'in a manner worthy of the gospel' (verse 27). What did this mean to the Philippians? What does it mean for you?

Widening our horizons

1 What is it about Christianity that often makes it thrive under persecution? Does it also indicate something about what human beings are like? Look up the history of church-Nazi relations.

Why, with some notable exceptions, did Hitler manage to muzzle and weaken the church at a time when the church should have been engaged in prophetic witness?

2 Paul's life was characterised by single-mindedness, a high level of personal commitment and great tenacity. Do people today display these qualities? If so, are they for good ends or for bad (personal ambition, power, self-aggrandisement)?

3 Consider the following attitudes to death. Show how each could be seen as Paul's attitude in verse 21, but is actually a corruption of it:
(a) 'This world is such a dreadful place that I don't want to bring children into it at all' (a childless couple who don't intend

to have children).
(b) 'This world is such a horrible place that I plan to end it all to be in heaven' (a teenager in turmoil).
(c) 'I am going to burn out, not rust out. If I die prematurely, so be it' (an older Christian).
(d) 'You don't have to die. You can achieve physical immortality — by removing from your total being the death consciousness, developing cellular connection with other immortals and accepting the possibility of immortality as a total new reality' (a New Age follower).

4 It would seem as a redeemed people, Christians are better placed to serve the wider community than others. Are they? *Do* they? Think about:
(a) Neighbourhood Watch
(b) social work and welfare agencies
(c) organisations committed to returning money to Third World manufacturers
(d) ecological or environmental groups
(e) Amnesty International.

To what extent can we work in such ventures wholeheartedly without compromise?

3
The best example of faith

How can we follow Jesus' example?
PHILIPPIANS CHAPTER 2, VERSES 1 TO 13

THE MAIN THEME OF THIS BOOK — persistence in faith whatever the odds — has as its centrepiece the hymn-like passage of Christ emptying himself for us to be found in verses 6 to 11. In doing this, Paul says, Jesus is an example of how we can live for him.

Living for others (verses 1 to 5)
When Paul writes in verse 4 that we should look to each other's interests and not merely to your own, his words take us to the heart of Christian living.

Paul himself confirms the centrality of this

thought by the way he connects it in verse 1 with the central Christian experiences of being loved, united in the Spirit, sharing and affection. The connection is made very close in verse 2: since his readers have already enjoyed these Christian experiences, they ought to affirm this oneness by thinking alike.

And if we are to regard others better than ourselves (verse 3), then it is but a short step to looking to their interests (verse 4). Paul's statement in verse 4 reflects certain elements of Jesus' teaching: the parable of the good Samaritan in Luke 10, verses 29 to 37; Jesus' own summary of the meaning of the law in Luke 10, verse 27 ('Love the Lord your God with all your heart. . . and your neighbour as yourself'); the parable of the last judgement (at the end of which Jesus said, 'Just as you did it to one of the least of these who are members of my family, you did to me'); and Jesus' teaching on greatness (where he says in Matthew 20, verse 26: 'Whoever wishes to be great among you must be your servant').

The message Paul has for his friends at Philippi is that living for others is the heart of the Christian life. Just how central that teaching is can be seen from the way in which Paul argues the point.

What is at the heart of living for others? The cross of Jesus. What does that reveal? The self-giving love of the Son of God, who laid no claim to equality with God, but made himself nothing. He gave himself away and died upon the cross (verses 5 to 11). Living for others is at the heart of the Christian faith because that's how Jesus lived — and died.

Jesus himself expressed this reality in prospect in Mark 10, verse 45: 'For the Son of Man came not to be served but to serve, and to give his life a ransom for many.' If, in seeing Jesus, we have seen the Father (John 14, verse 9), then we safely infer that Jesus was like that because God is like that.

Paul pulls out all the stops here to make sure this point is heard. There can be no more moving appeal to live the Christian life than this: Paul connects the believer's daily living directly with the death of Jesus!

He quotes from an early Christian hymn. In effect, what he's saying is: 'You know this truth; don't just hear it — *believe* it. You sing this truth in worship; don't just sing it — *live* it. This is what you have received; this is what you must also *give*. This is how Jesus acted towards you; this is how you must live in your dealings with *others*. Look to each other's interests and not merely to your own.'

Putting theology to work (verses 5 to 11)

We have now reached the most profound — as well as most moving — passage in this letter. In verses 5 to 11, Paul writes a hymn of praise, describing the mystery of the incarnation (verses 6 to 8). Then Paul soars to the heights of the glory which Christ has been given (verses 9 to 11) as he sums up the significance of the whole Christ-event — past, present and future — and its meaning for the life of the believer. These verses contain the deepest theology in the letter.

The word 'theology' needs explicating because it has actually developed a specialised usage which has crept into the English language in recent years. The word 'theology' is used, often in political circles, as a term of criticism and abuse. In parliament — whether in Westminster, Wellington or Canberra — to be accused of talking theology is to be accused of indulging in dull, meaningless talk!

This may be true of some of the more abstruse academic theologians, but it is hardly true of the apostle Paul. He may be mysterious at times, even difficult to understand, but never dull or meaningless, never theoretical or uninvolved in the business of living. This can be illustrated from the way he writes this deeply theological section of this letter.

The reason for such theology at this point in the letter is as practical and down-to-earth as it is possible to be. In verse 12 Paul says, 'Therefore... work out your own salvation with fear and trembling.' The Philippians are directed to Christ in his self-emptying love so that they may learn to *imitate* him and *live like him* in their relationships in the world. The theology is functional, the theory practical.

F. W. Beare says, 'The great hymn to Christ. . . is not primarily a formulation of Christological doctrine but a recital of the saving actions of Christ, put before us as the motive power of Christian living.'[21]

That is how it usually was with Paul. An interesting parallel is provided by his use of the same approach in the second letter to the Corinthians where he encourages participation in his scheme to raise a collection for the poor Christians in Jerusalem. In chapter 8, verse 9 he says: 'For you know the generous act of our Lord Jesus Christ, that though he was rich, yet for your sakes he became poor, so that by his poverty you might become rich.' Elevated theology, beautifully expressed and applied to. . . fund-raising!

Here in Philippians 2 similar themes, also poetically expressed, are given an equally practical objective: to encourage humility and unity in the hearts of the Christians at Philippi.

As Fred Craddock points out, the small issues raised in verse 5 'could be an indication that the church was suffering from the biggest problem of all: pettiness. . . The hymn stands. . . not only to define lordship and discipleship, but also as a judgement upon the kind of triumphalism that abandons the path of service and obedience.'[22]

Many commentators find the poetic feel of these verses significant — in fact, so much so that most commentators are in little doubt that Paul is here quoting a hymn, or part of a hymn, which would be familiar to his readers. Unfortunately, there has been little success in attempts to set the verses out in hymnic form, but fortunately we do not need to concern ourselves with the intricacies of Greek versification to appreciate the point which Paul is seeking to make.

Nor does it vitally affect the sense of the passage whether we believe that Paul is the author of the hymn, or is quoting a hymn composed by someone else. The fact that he used it allows us to be confident that he was endorsing its meaning and applying it as an argument to support what he wanted to say in his letter.

The lines of the hymn contain many ambiguous expressions which continue to be the subject of debate among scholars. What exactly is intended by phrases such as 'in the form of God', 'equality with God', 'emptied himself', 'taking the form of a slave', 'being born in human likeness'?

Many scholars argue that the hymn reflects and is influenced by the first century interest in Christ as the second Adam who, by reversing Adam's choice, also reversed its effects. Thus where Adam, created in the image of God, succumbed to the temptation to try to become as God, Christ did not regard his equality with God as something to be grasped and held onto. Instead, he chose to share the fate of humankind — slavery and death. God raised and vindicated him and that vindication will finally be displayed before every created being.

It may well be that while we approach the hymn with questions about the pre-existence of Christ, in fact the hymn itself begged those questions and developed only the contrast between Christ and Adam and the effects of their respective work. Thus allusively, suggestively Paul directs his friends to see that, in Fred Craddock's words, 'The central act in the drama of salvation is an act of humble service.'

There was no thought of personal profit in this act. Again, as Craddock says, 'The grave of Christ was a cave, not a tunnel. Christ acted on our behalf without view of gain.'[23] And just as Christ accomplished this by his obedience, so, too, must they — an exhortation which arises directly out of the meaning of the hymn. Christ's obedient service is the way which God has confirmed. His followers should not fear to imitate. The practical point which Paul was concerned to establish is affirmed.

Can hymns be taken seriously as theology? Some years ago now, in the days when radical theology flourished and some people were more keen to proclaim what they did not believe than to state what they did, a certain bishop was asked if he could recite the Apostles' Creed with a clear conscience. He replied, 'No, but I can sing it!'

While there is a serious strand to this statement, for the most part the answer was taken to demonstrate an attitude to worship which *devalues* praise and singing. The assumption is that the spoken word alone conveys the truth. The word sung may contain poetic licence — and therefore we don't need to be concerned about what we sing.

You can find such an attitude in churches. My own Presbyterian denomination used to be guilty of relegating everything before the sermon, especially the hymns, to the disparaging status of 'the preliminaries'! And while most churches have now repented of this error, you can still find congregations guilty of devaluing the praise in a worship service with little notes on the Order of Service, saying things such as, 'Latecomers please enter only during the singing of a hymn' — as though nothing of any significance was going on at this point, making the hymns a convenient time to disturb the congregation.

What may be objected to about this is that putting theology to music and so praising God is about the most worthwhile activity we can do as a community. Not only do we declare publicly our love for God; God also graciously uses music to edify us spiritually and strengthen us corporately.

You can see that being worked out in Paul's experience at Philippi. We have seen that when Paul and his companions arrived at Philippi, their mission encountered ferocious opposition and trouble. Acts 16 describes how Paul and Silas were imprisoned in Philippi as a result of their faith, but nevertheless affirmed their belief that God was with them. How? At midnight they were found 'praying and singing hymns to God' (verse 25), from which they derived strength and courage.

However, this dynamic is seen even more clearly at work in these verses in Philippians 2. In addressing a church which is undergoing difficulties and opposition, Paul is striving to encourage the humility and commitment to one another which he knows will be essential to the church's future survival and growth. He knows his friends are hard-pressed and will find this advice difficult, so he quotes this hymn they know, probably a hymn they use in their worship. The reason why he quotes a hymn is exactly the point just made: when we put theology to music, our hearts unite in praise of God and we are given strength.

Let's look at this further.

❑ *Our hearts unite in praise to God*
We need to remember that faith is not just a matter of the head — of believing or knowing certain truths cerebrally. Faith is also a matter of the heart — we are loved and have been redeemed by the death of the Son of God, as the Philippians hymn says. And our religious response is not just a matter of doing things we know to be right and proper; it is also a matter of *loving* the Lord who loved us and gave himself for us.

A religion of the head can be cold and unattractive at times — there is nothing so sterile as a dead orthodoxy. We also need the heart, the warmth of love. And verse 5 requires that, if properly translated.

I like the *Revised English Bible* here. It does not follow the line of translations which read something like, 'Have this mind among ourselves. . .' This suggests a religion of the head only. Rather, it translates this as 'Take to heart among yourselves. . .' — a translation which leaves open the place for emotion and warmth in the response which people offer to God for Christ's saving death.

There is an important point here. We need emotion in our faith; we need feeling. We need the commitment which flows from a heart which has been forgiven to a God who makes all things new. The British Methodist minister, Leslie Weatherhead of the City Temple, London, once said:

> What is wrong with emotion? If Christianity is falling in love with Christ, has anyone ever fallen in love without the deepest emotion. . . How could anyone come into contact with the living Christ and feel both his forgiving love and his relentless challenge without the very deepest emotion?

❐ *We are given strength*

Praise has a power to unite people — not just physically, as when a crowd sings with one voice, but emotionally. And praise also produces a deeper spiritual unity, when people affirm their shared values or outlook and know that they stand together.

The power the Civil Rights movement in the US in the 1960s was derived largely from one song, *We Shall Overcome Some Day*. Similarly, Paul sought to foster in his struggling movement a sense of unity and shared purpose by his use of the Christ hymn and the theology it expressed.

The pattern of Christ's life modelled a humility more concerned to serve than to be served (see Mark 10, verse 45). Paul set this pattern before his readers because he knew that a Christ-like humility would lead to a lively concern for others. So the key theology in the letter is focussed on Christ and is employed to incite the readers to Christian service in the world.

There was a similar marriage of deep theology and deeply practical purpose in the Barmen Declaration of the German Evangelical Church in 1934. It was drawn up to provide a common understanding, grounded in biblical and theological truth, about the church which would encourage Christians to resist Nazi encroachments. It was a protest at the attempts of the Nazis to secure church support for their program ('the national mission that God has given us') and virtually reduce the church to the level of an echo of government. This Declaration, like the hymn in Philippians, was modelled on Jesus.

After quoting John 14, verse 6 and chapter 10, verses 1 and 10, it declared:

Jesus Christ, as he is attested for us in Holy Scripture, is the one Word of God which we have to hear and which we have to trust and obey in life and death.[24]

These are not cheap words; many who subscribed to them paid for these words through persecution, imprisonment and death. But they provide a fitting and humbling example of the same principle that Paul attests in this section of the letter — that the life of the church and of individual Christians is to be modelled on the example of Jesus.

The Christ, of course, who humbled himself was also exalted by God and vindicated in the resurrection and ascension. If Christ's humility was the believer's example, then his vindication is the believer's encouragement. The powers of earth might look strong, but Paul is really saying that believers can have confidence that God's power is greater and will ultimately prevail. The conclusions he draws from that fact are developed in the next verses: 'Therefore, my beloved. . . work out your own salvation with fear and trembling, for it is God who is at work in you. . .' (verses 12 and 13).

Strength for all times (verses 12 to 14)

Paul wants to strengthen the faith of the church he dearly loves at Philippi. He does so by touching on the resources God offers to believers for living out their faith — experiences that cover the past, the present and the future.

☐ *God gives us strength from our past experience*

That is the force of verse 12. This points to the past commitments of the people — to the times, especially, when they committed their lives to Christ.

In effect, what Paul is saying to his friends is: 'Remember how you felt when you surrendered your life to Christ — the joy of belonging to Christ; the assurance of sin forgiven; the warmth of the love of the Christian fellowship; and the strength of the desire to live faithfully for Christ. Remember all that — and recover those feelings. Remember all that — and don't let the stream of faith get clogged and silted up with diversions.'

We don't know all of the details which led to the situation where the church at Philippi was in need of strengthening its faith. As we have seen, the account in Acts tells of the founding of the church at Philippi (Acts 16, verses 11 to 40). Paul's mission in Philippi had generated opposition and led to public disorder. Paul and Silas had been beaten and imprisoned and were asked — probably forced — to leave town. If Paul's experience at Thessalonica (see Acts 17 verses 1 to 10) was parallel to what happened in Philippi, then it is possible that after Paul and his companions had left the city, the opposition against Paul and the Christian message may well have been directed against the newly-formed church. The new Christians would then have been left to cope with community hostility without many resources or much support. This supposition gains some support from the references in chapter 1, verses 27 to 30 to the Philippians' struggle against opponents.

An alternative, more likely an additional source of difficulty is disclosed by Paul's mention in chapter 3, verse 2 of 'the dogs. . . the evil workers. . . those who mutilate the flesh.' This points to some controversy at Philippi over circumcision and therefore over the Jewish law. There is plenty of evidence in the New Testament to confirm the divisive and debilitating effect of such a controversy in a young congregation (see Galatians). A controversy along those lines could well have undermined the faith of many members of the church and led to the disunity against which Paul warns (for example, in chapter 2, verses 2 and 14)

However, the disagreement between Euodia and Syntyche which Paul deals with in chapter 4, verses 2 and 3 appears to be as much a personality clash as anything else and may be evidence of a congregation experiencing all the normal highs and lows of human relationships — the disagreements which arise at some time or another within most fellowships. Thus it may simply be that the routine passage of time has led to a dimming of vision and a loss of enthusiasm. That can certainly be a problem in the Christian life.

Relationships and commitments can become

clogged up with the passage of time. Other things intrude, other issues crop up and squeeze our discipleship out of its place of priority.

We lose some of the depth of our commitment in little, unseen ways at first — but then the slide becomes stronger, more obvious, and soon our commitment is visibly faltering. You can see it just as easily in a human relationship. We are busy at work, and we get tired; we neglect the little courtesies which love delights in; we take each other for granted; we forget to be appreciative. If we're not careful, our relationship can soon be stagnating and in a state that leads to trouble.

So, too, in the relationship of faith. The rot may set in unobtrusively, in little ways. It's not that we give up after some crisis of faith; we simply let our love grow cold and our faith slip away.

There must have been something like that going on in the church at Philippi and Paul was determined to stop the rot. His approach is similar to the one adopted by the risen Christ towards his church at Ephesus in Revelation 2, verse 4: get back to where you started; remember the warmth of your first commitment, the glow of your first love.

It is a sound strategy for a church facing times of difficulty. Remember your past experiences, reaffirm them and receive the strength which they offer.

An example of what this may mean comes from

one person's experience in a traumatic episode in the history of the church in Scotland. In 1843, the Church of Scotland was split as 474 ministers and thousands of members of the church left to form a separate denomination. For the ministers, this involved giving up church, home, stipend and many relationships with members who had decided not to leave the church. The ministers formalised their resignation by signing a document in Edinburgh.

Here is a contemporary record of how it worked out for one such minister:

> He came to Edinburgh, signed the Deed of Demission and set out — it was a long day's journey — to travel home on foot to that family whose home and whose support he had signed away. He entered a house by the wayside. As he crossed its threshold, the remembrance suddenly flashed upon him that it was thirty years since he had entered that door, going into Edinburgh to college, a solitary and friendless youth. Quickly upon that memory the thought of piety linked itself. 'The God,' said he to himself, 'who has hitherto guided me and mine these thirty years will not forsake me now.' His faith in his heavenly Father put fresh strength into his heart, and he went on his way with a light and elastic step.

I like the way the man's fear for the future was quelled by the remembrance of God's past faithfulness.

That is exactly the dynamic which Paul is trying to release into the church at Philippi: your past contains experiences of being helped. Draw on those experiences and re-live the help you have received. God is willing to give us strength for all times – including from our past.

☐ *God gives us strength from our present experiences*
One of the great incentives to Christian living should be the fellowship which ties Christians to one another in the church. Paul touches on that when he refers the church to his absence from them in verse 13. He's reminding them of the fellowship they share in Christ, of the way they depend on each other. That, too, is a factor in strengthening faith.

Paul was particularly close to the Christians at Philippi. There was a warmth between them and a mutual commitment to each other that both Paul and they found enriching and strengthening. Even when separated, they could still share joy with one another.

What Paul is doing, in effect, is to say, 'When your faith falters, don't let it. The strength of fellowship can be an incentive to strengthening faith. There are people who depend on you and on your faithfulness — don't give up; don't let them down.'

Our dependence on others and their dependence on us can be a strengthening factor. Many societies and self-help groups exist for just such a purpose.

People share a common background, experience or need and feel that they belong together and can help support one another. The Christian church is — or can be — an extended family and we can give and receive mutual support in it.

Let me illustrate from the experience of the one-time Dean of Johannesburg, Gonville Ffrench Beytagh, who was imprisoned in the 1960s in South Africa. The one thing that kept him going, he said, was the knowledge that his congregation was praying for him. Others were praying for him — that gave him strength. Others depended on him — that gave him courage. That's fellowship-strengthening faith.

☐ God gives us strength for the future

There is a future dimension in verse 13: '. . .for it is God who is at work in you, enabling you both to will and to work, for his good pleasure.' The possibilities before believers are unimaginable because God is at work in them.

Dr Edgar Elliston is assistant professor of leadership at Fuller Theological Seminary, California, and wrote recently about his experience when he was being sent to open up an extension facility for the seminary in Nigeria. He was apprehensive, in a heavily Muslim country, about clearing customs with cases of Christian books and resources.

His last stop before Nigeria was Amsterdam and, waiting at the airport there, he was approached by an elderly Nigerian who engaged him in conversation –

where he was going, what he was planning to do and so on. It turned out that the man was a retired civil servant from Nigeria who was returning from Costa Rica to take the very course that Elliston was setting up.

Prior to retirement, he had worked in customs and immigration and, when they reached Nigeria, he helped him through customs, smoothing out the awkward moments and dealing with the difficult questions to facilitate customs clearance.

Elliston thus discovered that his worries were unnecessary: God was already present and at work in his situation.

Many believers have had similar experiences — not necessarily dramatic, certainly not removing the requirement on them to be faithful and committed in their calling, but enough to give them encouragement that God is with them and at work in their situation. The realisation of that truth can be a tremendous encouragement and open up untold possibilities.

Discussion questions

Talking it through

1 Christian churches are often marked by divisions, rancour, pettiness and rivalry. Paul urged the Philippians to 'be of the same mind... the same love' (verse 2).

How does a common purpose and attitude help minimise the above threats to true fellowship? Why is 'selfish ambition or conceit' (verse 3) the opposite of love?

2 People often imagine that if everyone knew God, all the world's problems would be solved. Would they?
(a) How can power structures in the church as well as elsewhere debase people and sever relationships?
(b) How is Paul's advice 'in humility to regard others as better than yourselves' (verse 3) a helpful corrective to the abuse of power?

3 Think about the humility of Jesus (verses 5 to 11). How is humility different from putting yourself down? Was Jesus' humility imposed on him or voluntarily undertaken?

4 What in practical terms does it mean to 'work out your own salvation with fear and trembling' (verse 12)? If it doesn't mean relying on self-effort, what does it mean? See verse 13.

Widening our horizons

1 How can each of the following be the means of serving others:
 (a) the home
 (b) the church
 (c) the local community
 (d) the nation?
   In each case, think of at least one practical way to do so. What sacrifice would need to be made in each case? Is it worth it?

2 What is your view of the way advanced countries are cutting back on aid to less developed parts of the world? How can waste be avoided and we still carry out Jesus' instruction to serve others?

3 'Confidence in the future comes from affirmation in the past and the present.' With this in mind, how can the following activities give us confidence for the future:
 (a) remembering the specific acts of kindness and generosity that have been done for us by others
 (b) listing the specific skills, given to us by

God, that have proved useful in the past
(c) recognising the specific ways God has blessed us when we least expected or deserved it?

4 A contemporary expression is 'servant leadership'. What do *you* think this means? Compare verses 5 to 11 with John 13, verses 12 to 16.

Why is such a leadership style:
(a) so rare?
(b) so necessary?

4
People of faith

How can we put faith into action?
PHILIPPIANS CHAPTER 2, VERSES 14 TO 30

IGNACIO MARTIN BARO WAS a gifted, dedicated Christian — a man of grace and faith with the courage of his convictions. He offered for the priesthood in Spain, became a Jesuit missionary, taught social psychology at an overseas university and pastored poor people in the villages near the city where he worked.

When civil war broke out, his faith took practical expression — he taught the villagers first aid, a necessary skill for victims of war. He loved his work, caring for the people and serving God with little recognition or reward.

He now has both recognition and reward. In November 1989, Father Baro was one of the six

Jesuits in El Salvador dragged out of bed one Thursday morning and brutally killed. Their fate shocked and saddened people all over the world, reminding us all that what Dietrich Bonhoeffer called 'the cost of discipleship' can, for many Christians, be a high one.

We would probably never have heard of Father Baro, except for the terrible events in El Salvador. He was active and faithful — along with countless Christians, he was living out his faith. The events in which he was unexpectedly caught up enabled others to glimpse that faith. This section of Paul's letter gives us a similar glimpse of faith — this time among the early Christians at Philippi and elsewhere.

Christians at Philippi (verses 14 to 18)

Most Christians are not called upon to be faithful to death, but all Christians are called to be faithful. Paul affirms this in his instructions to his friends: 'do all things without murmuring or arguing, so that you may be blameless and innocent' (verses 14 and 15). Three things are noticeable here.

First, Paul's expectation was that being a Christian involved a tangible difference from the lifestyle of the surrounding society: the Philippians, Paul said were to 'shine like stars in the world' (verse 15). The metaphor is similar to one Jesus used in Matthew 5, verse 14 in the Sermon on the Mount: 'You are light for all the world.'

The source of the distinctive lifestyle of the Christian is Jesus himself, 'the light of the world'. Paul had already acknowledged in verse 12 that his friends had been living a life of Christian discipleship. He wanted them to continue, to persevere in their discipleship as they had been doing thus far.

These verses enable us to catch a glimpse of one way in which the life of discipleship is sustained. There are various echoes of the farewell speech of Moses to the Israelites before they entered the promised land, most especially the reference to 'a crooked and perverse generation' (verse 15) — an echo of Deuteronomy 32, verse 5.

In contrast to Moses' expectation that the Israelites would fall from the standards he had taught, Paul encouraged the Philippians to remain faithful. The contrasting expectations would supply a strong incentive! But notice: Paul obviously expected his hearers to catch the biblical allusion; they were evidently sufficiently well-grounded in the scriptures. That little detail provides an indirect reminder of the resources available for our Christian discipleship in the Bible.

This life of witness which Paul encouraged has evangelistic potential. It is by the Christians at Philippi holding fast to 'the word of life' (verse 16) that they were to witness effectively. The distinctiveness of their lifestyle would lead others to ask its source and open up opportunities to talk about Jesus. According to Jim

Wallis, one of the founders of the Sojourners Community in Washington, DC, this issue is 'the one central problem we face in the churches today'. His comment is worth pondering in full:

> The evangelism of the church has no power when the essence of the gospel is not lived out in the world. Peter, writing to the early Christians said, 'Always be prepared to make a defence to anyone who calls you to account for the hope that is in you' (1 Peter 3, verse 15). Which is to say, always be ready to explain yourself.
>
> When Peter told the early Christians to be prepared to answer for their faith, he was making an assumption that we dare not miss. He assumed that certain questions would be asked of Christians: 'Why do you people live the way you do? It's a mystery to us. It's contrary to our whole way of life. So what motivates you?'. . .
>
> The power of today's evangelism is tested by the question, What do we have to explain to the world about the way we live? But that question is no longer being asked of Christians. No-one is asking why we live the way we do. . . We have lost that visible style of life which was evident in the early Christian communities and which gave their evangelism its compelling power and authority.[25]

Paul's own situation had already provided an example of the way in which faithful Christian living could have evangelistic potential. He records in chapter 1, verses 12 to 14 how the fact that he was in prison for his faith had become common knowledge and had raised interest in Christianity. This gave other Christians opportunities to discuss and commend their faith.

Throughout the letter there are many passing references to the distinctive lifestyle to which Christians are called. Paul commends a manner of living which operates in the manner described by the American writer Paul Thoreau:

> If a man does not keep pace with his companions, perhaps it is because he hears a different drummer. Let him keep step with the music that he hears, however measured or far away.

Some of the topics to which Paul refers in this letter touch lifestyle issues which could provide modern Christians with opportunities to commend their faith.

For example, in the face of excessive and often selfish individualism, which has been rampant in Western cultures in recent decades, Paul's concern for unity and mutual support (as in Philippians 1, verse 27, chapter 2, verse 21 and chapter 4, verse 2) and his own personal desire to put the good of the Philippians before his own preferences (as at chapter 1, verses 23 to 26 and chapter 4, verse 17) highlight a quality of relationships quite out of step with the times! One might also include in this his appeal for humility and concern for others (chapter 2, verse 4ff.).

And Christians would surely have been asked for an explanation for their behaviour during the so-called 'greedy decade' of the 1980s if they had lived by Paul's instructions to avoid excessive consumption (chapter 3, verses 17 to 21), and practised the virtues of contentment and dependence on God (chapter 4, verses 12 and 13).

Paul was in no doubt that the Christian faith was for living, and he was not afraid to encourage his friends to take his own pattern of life as an example of how to live (chapter 3, verse 17 and chapter 4, verse 9). This was because his own life was modelled on Jesus Christ (see 1 Thessalonians 1, verse 6). Paul believed that the connection between his own life and the example of Jesus was so close he could actually sum up the pattern of Christian living which he commended as 'my ways in Christ Jesus' (1 Corinthians 4, verse 17). Modern Christians who followed in his footsteps would certainly stand out in the crowd, and would soon be asked to explain what made them tick!

Second, the test of faith, surprisingly, is how we cope with apparently minor details of daily living — lack of grumbling and argument, for example (verse 14). The needy neighbour, the confused teenager, the difficult colleague fall into this category.

That was Simon Peter's experience. 'Lord,' he said to Jesus, '. . .I will lay down my life for you' (John 13, verse 37). I do not doubt that. I doubt neither that Peter meant what he said, nor that Peter would have carried it out had the opportunity presented. There was a bold, brave, act-first-ask-later quality to Peter's discipleship.

But Peter's tragedy was that such heroics of discipleship were not required. What was required was something much smaller, but much more difficult. He had to face, not a capital charge, but a curious question from a casual bystander: 'You are one of this man's disciples, aren't you?' Peter's failure, later to haunt him bitterly, is a salutary reminder to all Christians of the importance of the small acts of loyalty, the lesser details of our life of discipleship. Paul did not want his friends at Philippi to neglect those.

Third, these verses allow us to see something of the rich fellowship the Christian life offers. Paul has already indicated that he might not return to his friends and the theme of the absence/presence of the apostle is touched upon at several points in this letter — verses 7 and 25 onwards (chapter 1) and verses 12 and 24 (chapter 2). We know from this letter and others Paul wrote — in I Corinthians 4, verse 15 for instance — that he took a fatherly interest in his churches and their development, using his relationship with them as an incentive to Christian living.

Their Christian development was not to be hindered

by his absence, but that did not mean he was not involved with them, nor they with him. Indeed, if Paul's impending trial were to end in his death, his life would be being poured out as 'a libation over the sacrifice and offering of your faith', while their faithful Christian living would make them Paul's 'boast on the day of Christ that I did not run in vain' (verse 16).

There's a relationship here, an interdependence between apostle and people, church leader and congregation, that we often don't fully affirm — or perhaps even accept? — in our modern Christian groups. If we did, I think we would find our life together immeasurably richer.

Paul and Timothy (verses 19 to 24)

Paul's confinement in prison did not confine his concern for his beloved church at Philippi. He wanted news of how things were going with them and he was confident that the news would be good and it would cheer him up to receive it (verse 19). These verses allow us a glimpse of Paul's faith by letting us see how he treated the individuals and the churches with whom he was involved. They reveal some facets of Paul's style of Christian leadership.

Paul could be tough when he felt he had to and he always felt he had to when a question involving the gospel was involved, as in Galatians, or when some issue of fundamental significance was at stake, as with the Corinthians. In these verses in Philippians he is quite blunt about some of his companions — verse 21, for instance. Incidentally, there were in the church many whose faith was new and raw. The New Testament church was a mixture of mature and immature, not a fellowship of those who were already perfect.

Paul, however, could also be warm and loving, as he is here, accentuating the positives and seeking to encourage and build up. He continues to trust his friends with his own hopes and fears about his situation. He is willing to disclose his own vulnerability.

Some scholars are perplexed about the lack of consistency in Paul's thinking about his own case: at one moment he appears uncertain what will happen to him (as in chapter 1, verse 27), at another he appears resigned to the likelihood of death (as in chapter 8, verse 17), while there are other passages where he seems confident that he would live and return and see his friends again (as in verse 24 here).

Any difficulty caused by this apparent inconsistency is resolved if we think in terms of a close relationship of mutual trust, of a friend talking to friends and sharing the fluctuations of mood which come to all who are encountering times of difficulty. Paul was not afraid to let his vulnerability show. His purpose was to show encouragement and see his friends grow in their faith.

Paul acted in a similarly encouraging way in his dealings with individuals, as his treatment of

Timothy here shows. Timothy first appeared as a disciple at Lystra, possibly a convert of Paul's preaching (if the father/son analogy here in verse 22 bears the same weight as it carries in 1 Corinthians 4, verse 15). He was sent back to Thessalonica as a representative of — even a troubleshooter for — Paul, after the apostle's hurried departure from that city.

He was used in a similar role during the troubles at Corinth, although some commentators think that they can read between the lines of 1 Corinthians 16, verses 10 and 11 a suggestion that Paul had doubts about Timothy's likely effectiveness. Then, of course, the letters which bear his name include the exhortation (in 1 Timothy 4, verse 12) to rise above the limitations which his youthfulness might impose on his ministry.

Yet Timothy was also a proven Christian worker — his record was known to the Philippians (verse 22) and his concern for the Philippians was obviously genuine (verse 20). He is named in verse 1 of this letter as its co-author and it is clear that, despite any inexperience, he is a Christian growing in faith and service through his involvement with Paul in his mission.

Like the servant in Jesus' parable in Luke 19, verse 17, he develops in service through the service he has already rendered. We are allowed to catch a glimpse of his growth and progress through the detail of this section of the letter.

Epaphroditus (verses 25 to 30)

It was only the searchlight of world attention that gave us a glimpse of Father Baro's faith — in or out of the limelight, he was faithful. In that respect, he was very like Epaphroditus in Philippians 2. Epaphroditus was active in the church which Paul had founded at Philippi. He had gifts which made him a suitable choice to be the agent of the church at Philippi in helping Paul and he had given splendid service to Paul.

He was faithful, he was active, he was committed — but we would never have heard of him, except that the searchlight of history caught him in its beam for a brief moment. It shone upon all the mundane things that real letters usually contain — details about health, travel arrangements and the need for TLC, as well as a glimpse of his faith.

Paul described Epaphroditus as 'my brother and co-worker and fellow soldier, your messenger and minister to my need' (verse 25). That is, in fact, a translation of five words in Greek, every one of which touches on some aspect of Christian faith and living. Just how central these aspects of Christian living are may be seen from the fact they are often the ones which are mentioned in the vows people take when they become members of the church today.

'Brother' refers to being part of the family of faith — the family united under God as Father and Jesus as Saviour and Lord; 'co-worker' touches upon service, which church members affirm when they promise to use their time, talents and money in the church's work in the world; 'fellow soldier' could refer to the struggle to maintain a Christian witness before others — the fight for truth, faith and love, along the lines of Ephesians 6, verses 10 to 20; 'messenger' is, literally, 'apostle', the same Greek word which Jesus used when he told the disciples, 'as the Father sent me, so I *send* you' (John 20, verse 21). Thus it covers both the Christian's mission in the world and his dependence on Jesus Christ.

Lastly, 'minister' is the Greek word *leitourgos*, which we still use in an English word like 'liturgy'. But for the Christian, liturgy or worship is not just what happens in church – it is that, certainly — but also the offering of all that we are to the Lord who gave his all for us.

Epaphroditus would have been faithful whether we had heard of him or not. There's food for thought in this for us. We should honour people like Paul, Timothy and Epaphroditus — and Father Baro. We have been able to catch a brief glimpse of their faith as the spotlight has caught them in its beam.

What matters is not whether we are seen and our faith makes headlines. God sees; God knows. Each Christian should resolve to be faithful in the task that God has given us with joy and gladness. And it may be that, by God's grace and perhaps without our knowing it, someone may catch a glimpse of that faith and decide to emulate it.

Discussion questions

Talking it through

1 'Blameless and innocent. . . without blemish in the midst of a crooked and perverse generation' (verse 15).

Is this a viable option for Christians today or an unrealistic expectation? Does it mean Christians are to be unreflective and naive? Compare Matthew 10, verse 16.

2 What does it mean to 'hold fast to the word of life' (verse 16)? How can this be expressed in daily living?

3 Think of Paul's young helper, Timothy (verses 19 to 24). How do you imagine him to be — what qualities of character, what temperament, what personality?

Why, do you think, did Paul have such a natural affinity with him?

4 Epahroditus is also a good role model (verses 25 to 30). Conscientious and loyal, he nearly died on his errand of mercy. Compare chapter 4, verse 18.

What does his experience tell us about the nature of Christian service? Must it always be at a personal cost? How can we more effectively honour those who work for and within the Christian community?

Widening our horizons

1 Paul presents Christianity as a lifestyle commitment. Look at *one* way in which being a Christian might affect your behaviour in these apparently unrelated areas of daily life:
 (a) maintaining your garden
 (b) driving your children from one place to another
 (c) playing sport
 (d) commuting.

2 Should a Christian's lifestyle be totally different from that of the world around us? Indicate any one way in which a Christian will have a distinctive attitude to each of these:
 (a) the economic future of society
 (b) forgiveness of those who have wronged us
 (c) the needy who cross our path
 (d) commitment to carving out a career path.

How do we best measure Christian distinctiveness — by what we think or what we do?

3 Why are we often more influenced by a person's actions than their stated beliefs? Which of the following influences us more:
   (a) a politician's policy statements or his treatment of his wife?
   (b) a preacher's statements from the pulpit or his dipping into the public purse?
   (c) a Christian's claim to love his fellows or his argumentative nature?

   Are our instincts right in making the judgments we do?

4 Why is being vulnerable to others essential if each of the following relationships is to work:
   (a) a marriage relationship?
   (b) a parent-child relationship?
   (c) a relationship between members of a church?

   Are there risks in sharing ourselves to all and sundry? When might this not be appropriate?

5
Expressions of faith

What is the basis of our faith?
PHILIPPIANS CHAPTER 3, VERSES 1 TO 21

PAUL CONCLUDES HIS COMMENDATION of Timothy and Epaphroditus in chapter 2 in the first verse of chapter 3. In the second half of that verse, he launches into a warning.

Fighting faith (verses 1 to 3)
We saw earlier that, when necessary, Paul could be vigorous in his denunciation when some fundamental gospel principle was at stake. There are certainly no punches being pulled by the apostle here! Those who tried to suggest that observance of the Jewish law was a necessary 'add-on' to faith in Christ found him vigorous in his disagreement and trenchant in his opposition.

It seemed that, like many other places that Paul visited, the church at Philippi had been infiltrated by some Christians anxious to see the Gentile converts adopt obedience to the requirements of the Jewish law as part of their Christianity. Paul had already fought this issue theologically in his letter to the Galatians and the language Paul uses in that letter is, in places, blistered by the heat of the controversy.

Paul saw that, if we are reconciled to God through faith in Christ, then any attempt to add on anything had the effect of calling in question the efficacy of Christ's death for our reconciliation and, therefore, undermining it. Any add-on in effect took away the power of Christ's death to reconcile us to God.

It is because the effect of their position was so damaging to the central truths of Christianity that Paul was so outspoken: fundamental issues were at stake and, while he could weep over false teaching (as in chapter 3, verse 18), he could also be implacable in his opposition to it. It would not be an exaggeration — as the letter to the Galatians shows — to say that Paul hated the false teaching which tried to *add on* the Jewish law to the cross of Christ.

'Hate' is a word we often feel uneasy about. Some may feel it inappropriate in a discussion about a religion which speaks so much about love. But I think that Paul's reaction here shows that there are times when Christians need to resist wrong —

whether in teaching or in living — as vigorously as possible and, if the wrong is sufficiently serious, actually to hate that wrong.

That certainly was Gonville Ffrench-Beytagh's view. As a result of his experiences combatting the excesses of apartheid in South Africa, he grew to understand that some things can be so wrong that the only option open to Christians is to oppose the wrong resolutely and try to overcome it. He wrote:

> Hatred is a theological word; it is the antithesis and complement of love. If you love someone or something very much, you must hate that which destroys the beloved, and the Bible is very clear about the many things that God hates. (I think that Christians are far too apt to try and escape from the need truly to hate evil, so that their love is wishy-washy and weak.)[26]

I think that Paul would have instinctively understood and agreed with this view.

Retrospective faith (verses 4 to 9)

We can sometimes find that our perspective on events changes when we are able to look back and review them with the benefit of hindsight.

In one of my favourite novels, Jane Austen's *Pride and Prejudice*, this is certainly the case. By the end of the novel, Elizabeth is able to regard D'Arcy in a much better light after she is able to overcome her initial prejudice against him. She then finds that she had misinterpreted him — and many of the motives and actions of which she had simply presumed he was guilty. Things appear very different when viewed with the benefit of hindsight.

That was Paul's experience — about life and religion, about his career and his priorities. As he looked back and surveyed his past, he was very forthright about the way he now saw things in a new light. He used colourful language: his old priorities, he now realised, were garbage.

One of the domestic chores which I particularly enjoy is emptying the wastepaper basket from my study. I love to get rid of all the 'garbage' there — used envelopes, letters I don't need to keep, phone messages I've dealt with and, above all, the working papers and notes from which last week's sermon was written!

Once useful, these papers are now trash: they can be thrown out. My wastepaper basket is full of things which used to be important to me, but are now being discarded. They are no longer important.

That's the point of view Paul is expressing here and he knew that the list of the things we no longer need and can easily afford to trash is huge. He maintained in verse 8 that everything *except our relationship with God through Jesus Christ* belongs in the garbage can.

In verses 4 to 6, Paul showed just how many

things he was willing to consign to the bin: his career, his social standing, his hopes and plans for the future, even his religion — which Paul took far more seriously than many people.

If Paul had been able to speak to the rich young ruler who came to Jesus (Mark 10, verse 17 onwards), that is what he would have told him: don't worry about the other stuff — your possessions, your social standing, your religion. It's garbage; it doesn't matter; get rid of it. Ultimately, from the viewpoint of eternity, everything except our relationship with God through Jesus Christ belongs in the garbage can.

For a moment the rich young ruler almost agreed. He took *life* seriously: he was not trapped by materialism into thinking that as long as he has enough to live on, then that was all he needed. He took *faith* seriously: he sought rigorously to keep the commandments of God. He took *Jesus* seriously: he was willing to throw his social standing to the wind as he ran up and admitted that Jesus held the key to the true meaning of life.

Mark 10, verse 21 says, 'And Jesus, looking at him, loved him' — loved him for the potential his life represented, loved him for who he was. Jesus said, 'You lack one thing; go, sell what you own, and give the money to the poor and... come, follow me.'

Hearing those words we can, like the disciples,

still react by asking questions about religion and wealth. That's valid and is part of the issue here. The man made it clear by his reaction that his money mattered more than anything else; money can be an important obstacle to true and satisfying faith.

For this man it was money: for others, as in Luke 9, verse 56 onwards, it could be material comfort or claims of family which were the distractions. For Paul, it was his religion and his career that kept him from finding God. The shape of 'the one little thing you lack' can vary from person to person, depending on lifestyle and attitudes, but in every life the 'one thing you lack' produces the same result — it keeps people from Jesus and following him.

We don't often hear the end of Jesus' sentence: 'come, follow *me*'. The one thing he lacked was Jesus Christ. And the one thing he could not do was leave other things aside and take Jesus Christ. That was the difference between the rich young ruler and Paul. He valued the other things more highly; Paul did not. If Paul could have met him, he'd probably have told him, 'These things are garbage. They don't last; they don't matter. Don't let them keep you from Jesus Christ. Everything except our relationship with God through Jesus Christ belongs in the garbage can.'

When he viewed his life in retrospect, that was what Paul saw — that was how he understood the impact which the risen Christ made upon his life.

Easter faith (verses 10 and 11)

Paul's belief in the reality of the risen Christ was central to his Christianity and he gave vivid expression to that in these two verses.

Paul had no doubt that Easter meant that Jesus rose from the dead on a given day in the past — he was at pains in 1 Corinthians 15 to remind his readers of that central reality. But, equally, he stressed that Easter is an on-going experience in the life of the believer. 'I want to know Christ and the power of his resurrection,' he wrote in verse 10, implying it is an event from the past that has present and future repercussions.

Paul spelt out part of what that means in these verses. The impact of Easter releases the power of the risen Christ into our lives and all things are made new. Paul knew what he was talking about — his encounter with the risen Christ was a dramatic, life-changing event.

But care is needed in reading this account. Paul alluded to Christ's power to change his life; it is easy to think, 'Yes, I know what you mean.'

For example, Augustine of Hippo, before he became a Christian, lived a life of self-indulgence, even when he knew he was on the wrong track. He prayed, 'O God, make me chaste, but not yet'! Then when he came to faith, he was utterly transformed.

The life of Francis of Assisi also displayed dramatic change, the product of a religious conversion.

Although historians are unsure whether it was the result of an experience of hearing a heavenly voice telling him to rebuild ruined churches, an exposure to poverty in Rome or an urge to identify with a begging leper, or some combination of the three, there is no doubt that his life was changed. From wealthy, pleasure-seaking self-indulgence, he moved to a life of preaching, penitence and poverty in imitation of Jesus Christ.

Now, to be sure, Christ did and does save people from situations of extreme need and transform them. But that was not Paul's experience; his experience was the very opposite: it was that Christ can save us from *the very best* that human life can offer. Indeed, if he is truly to save us, we must see that nothing is beyond his reach.

Paul in these verses was not bemoaning his lack of success as a Jew or as a Pharisee. Paul was not writing off his Jewish past as being of no value to him. He was a success; his past had held great value for him. It was not junk he threw away when he came to Christ; it was the very best he had going for him which suddenly *became* junk when he saw that it had no value compared to Christ.

What Paul experienced at the time of his conversion others have experienced at other stages in the Christian life. Careers, ambitions and even perspectives on life have been seen in a new light when subjected to the Lordship of Jesus Christ. The Glasgow church where

I grew up recently had a student assistant minister who had given up a career as a university professor of law to train for the Christian ministry. He had found life as a profesor, even a professor who was also an active Christian, unsatisfactory. He explained:

> For so long as I continue to have mental energies I should prefer to be devoting them to preparation for the exposition of the permanent gospel. . . And for so long as I continue to have physical and emotional energies, I should prefer to be devoting them to seeking to meet the spiritual and emotional needs of a congregation. . .[27]

Gerald Hawthorne sums up the conviction Paul is expressing by saying 'no person profits who does not surrender to Christ, and no person loses who surrenders everything to Christ'.

Paul's past success became irrelevant when he realised that he was using these things to try to win favour or standing in the sight of God — he was attempting to earn the right to be counted righteous in God's sight. But in the Easter event, God has triumphed in and through his Son. Christ has won full forgiveness and he offers it to all who put their faith in him. All other attempts to gain or earn acceptance in God's sight are, at a stroke, declared redundant and unnecessary.

The events of Easter were to make that clear: Christ had conquered; he was raised by God and given to his disciples as a risen presence and then, through the Spirit, as inner power — in order to strengthen, to make new, to transform. Think of the disciples in John 20: one moment huddling behind locked doors in fear, then, after encountering their risen Lord and being filled with power, commissioned to take on the world and win.

These words in verses 10 and 11 have power because many reading them know that where Jesus Christ is acknowledged as living Lord in a believer's life, similar transformations can occur, not just in people's weaknesses, but also in their strengths. He takes charge of priorities and gives new directions. He becomes the person in charge, the driving force, the director. He takes charge of a person's life.

I was talking recently to a man whose company had been taken over. He was finding work difficult when I spoke to him: his colleagues and he were all trying to adjust to the new corporate structure. They had a new boss who brought to bear his own personality on the organisation. The new management had different priorities and procedures, with the result that he and his colleagues had to adjust to a new way of doing things.

In a sense, faith is like that: it is being 'taken over' by Jesus Christ. Christian living is adjusting to the new goals and the new procedures of the new owner. As Paul described it in 2 Corinthians 5, verse 17: 'So if anyone is in Christ, there is a new creation: everything old has passed away; see, everything has become new.' Our life is under new management, and the new managing director has new resources and facilities, as well as the necessary expertise, to safeguard our enterprise.

The Covenant Service which started in the Methodist Church is direct and challenging on this matter. Part of the service includes these words:

> Christ has many services to be done: some are easy, others are difficult; some bring honour, others bring reproach; some are suitable to our natural inclinations and material interests, others are contrary to both. In some, we may please Christ and please ourselves; in others we cannot please Christ except by denying ourselves. Yet the power to do all these things is given us in Christ, who strengthens us.[28]

Christ is in charge. Christ is the Lord of our strengths, not just our weaknesses. That shows the impact of Easter, 'the power of his resurrection' (verse 10) in people's lives here and now.

In this way, Christians share in the power of Christ's resurrection now, looking forward to a fuller share in eternity. Verse 11 might suggest that Paul is hesitant and uncertain about this. Paul writes literally, '. . .if somehow I may attain the resurrection from the dead'. His seeming uncertainty is more apparent than real; it is caused by the construction of the Greek expression he uses. A look at verse 14 below — and at passages such as Philippians 1, verse 21 and chapter 2, verse 16 onwards — will clearly show that Paul's hope of sharing in Christ's victory over death was not a hesitant or uncertain one.

Perfecting faith (verse 12)

'Nobody's perfect' — that is one of the most common statements people make. We may use it to bolster our own *self-esteem*. For example, if someone is being praised too generously for our liking, we may mutter, 'Oh, come off it, she isn't that great. She's got her faults: after all, nobody's perfect.'

Or we may use it to cover for our own *weaknesses*. When we make a slip or fail in some way, we may shrug it off by saying, 'It can't be helped. There was nothing I could do. After all, nobody's perfect.'

We may even use it to describe our own *faith*. Most of us have moments when we know that we are not the people we ought to be or the church is not the sign of the kingdom God means it to be, but we banish this discomforting thought by saying, 'Too bad, but there's nothing you can do. After all, nobody's perfect.'

So it is comforting if we assume Paul is giving his apostolic blessing on such frames of mind. In this verse, he virtually says, 'I am not perfect.' We might almost expect him to agree with the coy windscreen sticker some people display on their cars, 'Christians aren't perfect, just forgiven'!

At one level it is profoundly true and a useful antidote to the common misapprehension in society that you can only come to God when you already have your act together, not needing to become integrated and whole. At another, it can be used to rationalise under-achievement or spiritual mediocrity.

But that's not what Paul meant at all. It is true that he implied that nobody's perfect. He certainly did admit that *he's* not perfect. But what follows from that is not along the lines of our attitude which rationalises our failures. With Paul, it was the very opposite: 'I know I'm not perfect *and I'm working on it*. I'm doing something about it!' He was saying, in effect, 'I'm not perfect — not yet — but I press on!' He was not prepared to remain at a spiritually immature level.

Notice how he described the process he adopted: 'I press on to make it my own, because Christ Jesus has made me his own.' In other words, the goal Paul was working towards was not his own plans for his life, but Christ's. Paul underscores as an important feature of the Christian life that the initiative and the direction lie with God and Christ: we are called to cooperate with God in developing our faith.

Paul had already spoken of this. In Philippians

1, verse 6, Paul spoke of 'the one who began a good work among you. . .', and in Philippians 2, verses 12b and 13, he could express both sides of the dynamic of faith – on the one hand, 'work out your own salvation with fear and trembling'; on the other, 'it is God who is at work in you, enabling you both to will and to work for his good pleasure'.

The reason people are Christians has fundamentally nothing to do with what they feel, wish or need — that does come into it, but only later. The reason is because God loves us, gave Christ to be our sacrifice and calls us to become like him.

This appears frequently in the New Testament as a work that God does: In Romans 8, verse 29, he said we are 'predestined to be conformed to the image of his Son'; in Galatians 4, verse 19, Paul described his work with the church as labouring until 'Christ is formed in you'; and in 2 Corinthians 3, verse 18, he said Christians 'are being transformed into the same image from one degree of glory to another'.

From verse 10 onwards of this chapter, Paul talked about knowing Christ, being changed by the 'sharing of his sufferings'. That gives us the clue as to what Paul meant by saying he is *not yet* perfect.

We tend to think of perfection as meaning something static: full, unimpaired moral purity. The New Testament sees perfection in much more dynamic terms, even when talking of Jesus himself.

In Hebrews 5, verses 8 to 9, the writer says, 'Although he was a Son, he learned obedience through what he suffered; and having been made perfect, he became the source of eternal salvation for all who obey him.'

Christ's perfection was not static, part of his nature when he came to earth; it was dynamic, growing, developing, expressed in his loving obedience to God step by step along the way to the cross. For Jesus, too, there was the process of dying to self and living to God. The Gospels show us some trace of this.

When Jesus was baptised, he heard God saying (in Mark 1, verse 11), 'You are my Son, the beloved; with you I am well pleased'. These words were first used in the Suffering Servant passages in Isaiah where there is the first suggestion of the cross. Jesus struggled with this for forty days in the wilderness. The central thrust of that experience of being tested was 'If you are the Christ. . .', then find some way other than the way of suffering, the way of the cross.

When Peter first confessed that Jesus is the Christ (Mark 8), but then tried to deflect him from the cross, Peter was rebuked (in verse 27): 'Get behind me, Satan!' This is followed by the experience of transfiguration, where the cross is confirmed as the route to be taken by the Son of God.

Then in the garden of Gethsemane (Matthew 26, verse 39), Jesus prays: 'My Father, if it is possible, let this cup pass from me; yet not what I want, but what you want.' Then even in Matthew 27, verse 42 on the cross Jesus is challenged: 'He is the King of Israel; let him come down from the cross now, and we will believe in him.'

At every stage, Jesus has to struggle to align his will with God's will, to develop his obedience to God in his life and ministry, actually to follow where the will of God directed. That was the way he became perfect – by learning obedience and implementing it. For his disciples, the pattern is exactly similar: leave self behind, take up the cross and come, follow me (Mark 8, verse 34).

That's why Paul talked here about his life as involving a growing conformity with Christ's death; that's why he often talked about dying to self and rising to newness of life with Christ.

A church once was asked to provide a home for a rubber plant. It had become too large for the office where it had been growing and, unless it could be housed in a larger space, it would die. The church can be a place where the people of God, just like that plant, find room to grow and where they express their desire to grow towards the perfection of Christ's image being reproduced in them.

Did Christ die so that we might remain the way we are? Was all the agony of the garden and the cross simply to endorse the status quo of our too-timid lives?

Christ has higher aims for us and deeper purposes. Through all we are and do, we are to develop a growing conformity to his death until we become like him (Hebrews 13, verses 20 and 21):

> . . .That to perfection's sacred height,
> We nearer still may rise,
> And all we think and all we do,
> Be pleasing in his eyes.

Forward in faith (verses 13 to 16)

A contemporary growth industry is the human potential movement. Whether one thinks individually, in personality or career terms, or corporately, in terms of the effectiveness of an organisation, the realising and releasing of one's full human potential is big business. Whether or not we agree with all the strategies advocated or the remedies suggested by the human potential movement, we would probably not argue with the basic premise that it's good to develop our full potential.

Developing our faith could well begin with these verses in Philippians 3. Paul writes in verses 13 and 14, '. . .forgetting what lies behind and straining forward to what lies ahead, I press on toward the goal for the prize of the heavenly call. . .'

Forgetting what is behind may seem a strange thing for Paul to say when he had just recounted the major features in his past life, making it obvious that he had not forgotten anything. But what he meant was that he ignores what is behind and he refuses to allow it to become a burden or a restriction on his Christian living now. Paul could not deny that he was all of the things he described in verses 5 to 8, but he could refuse to allow them to intimidate him or impede him in his life of faith. The past is now the past; thanks to Christ, it is over and done with. It can be laid to rest, even though the details may still be in the memory.

I remember the Rev. Jesse Jackson's final speech to the Democratic Convention of 1984 at which he had been unsuccessful in his attempt to gain his party's nomination for the presidential election held that year. Under a cloud because of past associations, he said, 'As I develop and serve, be patient. God is not finished with me yet.' Leaving aside the politics behind the statement, the point he made happens to be theologically correct and points to the process Paul is describing in these verses.

One thing that helped Paul lay to rest the past was that he was fully occupied in pressing towards the goal. Paul's words in verse 9 and following make it clear that the efforts to which he refers here are not works as a *condition* of being saved — doing good in order to be accepted by God — but works as a *consequence* of being saved — doing good because accepted by God. Paul's use of a metaphor from athletics reminds us that we can grow in faith only when we are prepared to work at it, bringing to our life of faith the same commitment, dedication and discipline that the athlete does to her training.

Alexander Solzhenitsyn uses the training metaphor in one of his 'prose poems':

> At sunrise thirty young people ran out into the clearing; they fanned out, their faces turned towards the sun, and began to bend down, to drop to their knees, to bow, to lie flat on their faces, to stretch out their arms, to lift up their hands, and then drop back on their knees again.
> All this lasted for a quarter of an hour.
> From a distance you might have thought they were praying.
> In this age no-one is surprised if people cherish their bodies patiently and attentively every day of their lives.
> But they would be jeered at if they paid the same regard to their souls.
> No, these people are not praying. They are doing their morning exercises.[29]

Prayer, worship, Bible study, a serious effort to let the Christ-like graces grow and take root in our lives — all these should be a regular part of our training for the Christian life.

Whether the athlete is the tennis player who has just won Wimbledon, the footballer whose team has just won the grand final, or the golfer who has just won the US Open, the question is invariably asked,

'What's next?' and the answer, equally invariably, is given, 'Well, there's always next year. . .' They look ahead and plan for the next challenge. The Christian life is intended to be a life of growth and development, building on the achievements which God has allowed us to make (verse 16) and trusting God to lead and direct our steps (verse 15) in accordance with the truth he has revealed.

It would be a mistake, however, to imagine that 'it all depends on me'. The goal is 'the heavenly call of God in Christ Jesus' (verse 14). God is — and wants to be — involved in every step along our road to maturity of faith.

Discussion questions

Talking it through

1 The apostle Paul was constantly having his ministry subverted by the circumcisers — the 'dogs', the 'evil workers', 'those who mutilate the flesh' (verse 2).

From where does the main attack on the gospel come today — from within the institutional church or outside it? What are some contemporary expressions of the idea that faith in Christ alone is not enough — that we need 'faith plus...'?

2 What point is Paul making in consigning his 'religion' to the garbage heap? See verse 8.

3 Paul's religious credentials were impeccable (verses 4 to 6). Yet they weren't enough. Why not? See verses 7 to 9. What was the source of Paul's confidence (verse 10)? How did this identification with Christ express itself?

4 Paul showed a refreshing candour about his own spiritual achievements (verses 12 to 14). What gave Paul the edge spiritually — what set him apart? Is this goal attainable by all or limited to a select few (verses 15 and 16)?

5 Think of the author's illustration of a company takeover (page 106). How does this explain the nature of the new ownership of the life of a Christian?

6 Philippians 3 offers the clearest statement of the apostle Paul's life-goal. Many Christians have made verse 10 their personal aim or ambition.

Are you able to sum up your aim in life in a single sentence? Does your life have this kind of focus or do you find yourself with a set of different, even conflicting aims? Share as honestly and openly as you can.

Widening our horizons

1 Using verse 12 as a resource, isolate the possible flaws in each of the following statements:
   (a) 'She'll be right!'
   (b) 'I always say No when I'm not sure.'
   (c) 'Nobody's perfect.'
   (d) 'Keep truckin'.'

2 Do you accept Ffrench-Beytagh's view (page 99) about the need to hate? If so, what precisely should be remembered, and what not, about each of the following:
   (a) the former system of apartheid in South Africa
   (b) the massacre of innocent civilians by their own governments
   (c) sexual abuse by a parent of his or her child
   (d) embezzlement or fraud by a person in a position of trust?

3 In the light of Paul's examination of himself in verses 4 to 9, how much do each of the following stand in the way of putting Christ and his agenda at the centre of your life:

(a) social position
(b) the good opinion of others
(c) work and prosperity
(d) social activities and holidays?

Is there any other factor that is a serious impediment to your being truly Christ-centred?

4 Which of the following statements most closely approximates your own reason for going to church:
(a) 'I go to church because I love its predictability. I feel most at home when I experience what I'm used to.'
(b) 'I go to church because, in worshipping with others, I am opening myself up to the possibility of change.'
(c) 'I go to church to worship God, not to be distracted by conversation with other people. That's why I don't like to stand around and engage in idle talk afterwards.'
(d) 'I go to church because I get really lonely and long to meet people with whom I can share my problems.'

What makes church come alive for you?

5 Paul appeals to the mature to 'be of the same mind' and 'hold fast to what we have attained' (verses 15 and 16). How does this add weight to the following aphorism?

> *In essentials, unity.*
> *In non-essentials, liberty.*
> *In all things, charity.*

6
Faithful leadership

What is the goal of faith?
PHILIPPIANS CHAPTER 3, VERSES 17 TO 21
AND CHAPTER 4, VERSES 1 TO 4

I WAS ONCE STANDING AT THE CHECKOUT of a large store. The customer in front of me tendered the wrong note to pay for his purchases and, in good humour, the shop assistant teased him by suggesting that he had deliberately tried to cheat her.

'You'll not go to heaven if you do things like that,' she laughed.

I was taken aback by his reply: 'When I see some of those who think they are going to heaven, I'm not sure that I want to go.'

This highlights the credibility gap between Christians' belief and their practice. One standard reaction to that this sad state of affairs is a marked modesty in the claims Christians make either for themselves or about the church. Implied in this modesty is the thought that people should follow Jesus and imitate him, not those of us who follow him.

There is good and bad theology here. The good theology is that it is indeed Jesus Christ whom people should follow and who should be acknowledged as Lord of the church. The bad theology is that this type of thinking may too easily encourage Christians to be complacent about their own underachievement. Even Christian leaders can settle for 'Do as I say, not as I do.' The logical conclusion is that the Christian faith is theoretical only; no-one should look for actual results in the life of the believer — and that surely is an absurd and unChristian position!

It is, of course, fundamentally true that Christ is the centre of the church and the Lord of the believer's life. But if what we saw above is true, about God wanting Christ's followers to grow into his image and become like him, then it should be possible for Christians — with proper safeguards for humility, of course — to point to features in their own lives and hold them up to others as models worthy of imitation.

In the verses that follow, Paul now tries to encourage development in the faith of his friends. He knows that, with good leadership, their faith will flourish; so he comments on his own leadership role and then tries to resolve a problem threatening the leadership of the church in Philippi.

Paul's style of leadership (verses 17 to 21)

These verses are startling and surprising. They challenge our understanding of the Christian life because Paul points to himself as a model. Quite unselfconsciously, he invites his readers (in verse 17) to 'join in imitating me, and observe those who live according to the example you have in us.'

Fortunately, Paul has already made clear in this chapter that the basis of his Christian life is Jesus Christ — his death, resurrection and indwelling power — so we know he was not putting himself at the centre of his faith. That would hardly square with his earlier comment, 'For to me, living is Christ.'

What Paul does here, though, is challenge us to take seriously all that he has been saying about the growth of faith in the believer's life. If we really do let Christ work in us, if we really do 'press on', then there will be marks of Christ in our lives, changes he has brought about, to which we can point others. And while we will — and must! — say, 'not I, but Christ', we should also be able to say, 'join in imitating me.'

The process which is involved here is well described in a prayer which Martin Luther King Jr used frequently: 'O Lord, I ain't what I ought to be and I ain't what I'm gonna be but, thanks to you, I ain't what I used to be.'

'For to me, living is Christ' actually allows us to see the centre of Paul's Christian life and to distinguish true religion from false. For Paul, Christ was the centre of his life and the focus of his priorities.

Other people have other 'centres', other priorities. Paul warns with sadness about a group of such people who are causing trouble at Philippi, whose behaviour made them 'enemies of the cross of Christ' (verse 18) and that actually 'their god is the belly' (verse 19).

That may seem just to be a metaphor, but it is more: it actually describes a dynamic of the religious life. We mentioned in chapter 1 Paul Tillich's definition of religion as 'the state of being grasped by an ultimate concern'. We saw that what he meant by this was that our lives are filled with might be proper and necessary concerns — for food, work, love and so forth — but that over and above all these concerns there is, in most people's lives, one over-arching and fundamental concern, one's religion.

For some people at Philippi it was their appetite: they treated matters of eating and drinking with an almost religious seriousness and devotion. For Paul, his ultimate concern was Jesus Christ and he encouraged his friends at Philippi to follow his example by making Jesus their ultimate concern.

One final encouragement and incentive is held out in verses 20 and 21. Here Paul contrasts the earth-bound, impermanent nature of the concerns he has rejected with the permanent, eternal quality of an authentic faith based on Jesus Christ. Now that could have been an excuse for escapism: pie-in-the-sky-when-you-die stuff. But in Paul's hands it is not: he was seeking to widen his friends' horizons and deepen their commitment by reminding them of the eternal dimensions to their discipleship.

The actress Helen Mirren when interviewed on her role in *Mosquito Coast* gave a parallel of this. She said that she wanted to give the character she was playing the same quality she saw in women from Lebanon whom she'd seen in a TV documentary. They were, she said:

> . . .going about their daily tasks: making sure the kids are fed, getting water to wash the clothes — the stuff that makes the world go round in the midst of war and famine. By their stoicism these women make sure there are going to be human beings in the next generation. They have a look in their faces that is indescribable. . . an extraordinary expression, as though they were looking 1,000 years ahead.

Isn't that a revelation: people keeping going in the routine duties of life — even amid war and destruction — by looking ahead. The Christian can look even further ahead than 1,000 years and be even more inspired. The citizens of heaven do not have 'their minds set . . .on earthly things' (verse 19) and are sustained by a power that is greater than anything else in the world — 'the power that also enables [Jesus] to make all things subject to himself' (verse 21).

If further proof is needed that Paul is speaking out of humility and genuine Christian concern, then verse 1 of chapter 4 provides it. He speaks there of love for and joy in his friends, he expresses longing to share again their fellowship and he declares that acting 'in this way' — in imitation of him — is the way to 'stand firm in the Lord'.

Leadership in the Philippian church (chapter 4, verses 2 to 4)

The role of women in the church is controversial in a number of denominations at the moment. In some churches, there are advocates for women's ordination trying to change church structures to *allow* women to minister as clergy. In other denominations, including my own where women have been eligible for the ministry of word and sacrament for years, the pressure has been to *take away* that eligibility.

There is a wide variety of arguments canvassed in the debate about the ministry of women. The advocates of women's ministry have to come to terms with a passage such as 1 Timothy 2, verse 11 onwards which seems to enjoin a passive and silent role for women in the church, at least as a short-term policy in the face of false teaching in the church of Ephesus.

Opponents of women's ordination, however, must also come to terms with several biblical passages which are at least as uncomfortable for their position, passages which show quite clearly that women *did* exercise leadership in the early church. This is one such passage and it makes the church at Philippi a central piece of evidence about the ministry of women in the early church. The church at Philippi, humanly speaking, owed a great deal to women.

Acts 16 shows that, when Paul arrived at Philippi, there was no Jewish synagogue in which he could preach and find a springboard for his mission. Apparently, there were less than ten Jewish males in town — the necessary minimum required to enable a synagogue to function. But there was faith in God at Philippi and there was Jewish worship. And it was nourished and kept alive by women.

The women met at a place for prayer down by the riverside. When Paul preached there, people came to faith, a church was formed and Lydia, one of the women who became a Christian, opened her house to give hospitality to Paul and his companions, providing a home for the infant church.

The church grew and became a loving, loyal support group for Paul and, when he wrote to them years later, we see among its leaders two women, Euodia and Syntyche. So Philippians provides an answer to the question about women exercising leadership in the church by showing that women could act — and did act — as leaders in the Christian church.

This matches what Paul wrote elsewhere. To the Galatian church, Paul wrote: 'There is no longer Jew and Greek, there is no longer slave or free, there is no longer male and female: for all of you are one in Christ Jesus' (Galatians 3, verse 28). This coincides with his other references to women in his letters, and to the roles which Acts shows us Priscilla (Acts 18) and the daughters of Philip (Acts 21, verse 9) exercised in the early church. The scripture shows that women exercised leadership in the church.

But our examination of the church at Philippi raises the more important question about leadership in the church, whether conducted by men or by women: is it *Christian* leadership? To examine that, it is necessary to think what distinctively Christian leadership would be. Let me offer a provisional statement as a working basis: 'Christian leadership is Christ's gift to the church, offered back to him and dedicated to his glory.'

Let's unpack this, with reference to the leaders at Philippi.

❑ *Leadership is Christ's gift to the church*
Lydia provides a useful model of someone who was

called by Christ. In Acts 16, verse 15 she said, 'If you have judged me to be faithful to the Lord, come and stay at my house.'

Her Christian service is her response to the grace, mercy and love of God in Jesus Christ. She served, offering what she could out of gratitude. Whether she became a leader or not, we do not know. But this willingness to serve is the first step.

Other women did become leaders and took a full share in the work of the gospel. Two of them (mentioned earlier) are named in our text, Euodia and Syntyche. Although we have no details as to who these women were, or how they came to be Christians, I'm sure the pattern was exactly the same for them: they came to faith and used their gifts in Christian service.

That is the way it usually happens. Nikolaus von Zinzendorf discovered that his life of faith and service began in an art gallery. He saw Domenico Fetti's painting of Christ on the cross, *Ecce Homo*. The artist had wanted his work to be a spiritual experience, not just an aesthetic one, and so had added an inscription to the frame of his painting: 'All this I have done for you; what have you done for me?'

This moved Nikolaus to commit his life fully to Christ and led, in time, to a life of dedicated service to missions. That is the pattern which makes both service and leadership 'Christian'.[30] All this was possible because Christ had called him and made of him a gift to the church.

❑ *Leadership is offered back to Christ*
When leadership and ministry are offered back to Christ, he can guide, enable and sustain our service. That needs to happen, for we are too prone to mistakes, short-sightedness and sin.

Rev. James Curry was a well-known Scottish minister: a popular, flamboyant man, he used his love of Robert Burns and Burns Suppers to reach people whom the church did not always manage to contact.

At one such supper, he spoke with great humour, but one man in the audience did not laugh at any of his jokes. On the way home, he was asked if he'd enjoyed Curry. He said he had. Asked if he hadn't thought him funny, he replied: 'I thought he was very funny, but I don't like him. I'll laugh when I go home.' That is a breathtaking example of human perversity – and it can happen as easily in the church as elsewhere.

It must have been something similar which led Euodia and Syntyche to have their disagreement. Had it been a major quarrel over the gospel, Paul would have corrected whichever one was in the wrong. Therefore we may assume that it must have been a personal difference over something insignificant, but it needed to be put right before it grew worse. So Paul said, 'be of the same mind *in the Lord*' (verse 2).

The effect of the words 'in the Lord' is to encourage the women to lay their disagreement before

Jesus. It is as though Paul had said, 'Submit your quarrel to Christ as Lord and let him decide the matter.' Unless this problem is solved, their work for God was going to be undermined and they would be unable to offer anything back to Christ.

❑ *Leadership is dedicated to Christ's glory*
That is *why* they had been working. Paul said that Euodia and Syntyche 'have struggled beside me in the work of the gospel' (verse 3). He included them among his 'co-workers' — a term which indicates preaching and evangelistic service — to judge from its usage in Romans 16, verses 3, 9 and 21, and Philemon, verse 24, for example.

Their service was to be directed towards the result of our faith — sharing eternity with God. Jesus' followers are citizens of heaven, as Paul has just said at the end of chapter 3. Euodia and Syntyche are among those 'whose names are in the book of life' (verse 2). That reminds us that God has created us and redeemed us 'to glorify him and enjoy him forever. . .' as the Westminster Confession says.

So we work together to bring others to faith in him, to express his love in action in people's lives. Our worship, our prayer, our study, our service — all is undertaken to bring glory to his name. This means that we need never lose heart: God is working his purpose out. We glorify not ourselves, not our church, but the Lord and Saviour of the church, Jesus Christ.

Where faith is in health, the desire for the glory of Jesus Christ is always paramount. When Swiss theologian Karl Barth turned seventy-five, he tried to make light of the congratulations and appreciation he received. He played down especially the expressions of praise he had received in the way he responded in the circular letter which he wrote to all who had sent him greetings or congratulations:

> To be famous ('the greatest scholar of our time' as I even read on the cake) is all very pleasant. But who will finally be praised? . . .Our whole office is to praise him from the depths as best we may.[31]

That is the Christian way — to praise God and bring glory to his name. The men and women who lead the church are Christ's gift to the church, offered back to him and dedicated to his glory.

Discussion questions

Talking it through

1 Paul could be accused of skiting or bragging (chapter 3, verse 17). Was he?

How is the example of other Christians still important today? How can we distinguish positive role-models from negative ones — the 'enemies of the cross' (chapter 3, verses 18 and 19)?

2 Paul loved to describe his converts in glowing terms of praise (compare 1 Thessalonians 2, verses 19 and 20 with chapter 4, verse 1). What does this show us about the apostle to the Gentiles?

From where do you derive your most profound sense of satisfaction?

3 Euodia and Syntyche — loyal companions of Paul, but quarrelsome colleagues, unable to get along.

What course of action does Paul suggest (verses 2 and 3)? What strategies have you seen work to resolve personality differences or conflict within Christian circles?

Do sometimes we just have to 'agree to disagree'?

4 In verse 4, Paul tells us to rejoice. What do you think Paul thinks there is to rejoice about?

Widening our horizons

1 Should there be a differentiation of roles between men and women:
  (a) in sports such as football?
  (b) in office employment?
  (c) in the leadership of a country?
  (d) in church leadership?
  (e) in leadership of the home?
  If you think there should be, what are your reasons?

2 Is leadership essential in life? What do you think would be the advantages and disadvantages of:
  (a) a team of workers building a car from beginning to end, each member having equal responsibility?
  (b) a church council where all decisions are by consensus?
  (c) an Ancient Greek city-state type government where all citizens have equal voting rights on all key issues?
  (d) a hierarchical corporate structure with vertical accountability and clear lines of responsibility?

3 If we come to the realisation that eternal life really exists, what effect can this have on:
  (a) our view of our own suffering?
  (b) our view of what we should do with our lives?
  (c) our view of others who don't believe that eternity exists?
  Should our lives be centred on the present or the future? Can it be both?

4 What principles could be used to protect each of the following from the 'cult of leadership':
  (a) the managing director of a company?
  (b) the senior pastor/minister/rector/priest of a church?
  (c) the captain of a sporting team?
  (d) the leader of a political party?

7
The bonds of faith

What are the rewards of faith?
PHILIPPIANS CHAPTER 4, VERSES 4 TO 23

PAUL WROTE THE LETTER to the Philippians in full awareness that he might be facing his 'final curtain', to use Frank Sinatra's expression in his song *My Way*. And now the time has come for Paul to draw his letter to a close. He has important things to say. He wants to state the case of which he is certain and leave his friends with a benediction for their Christian lives.

Paul's parting gift to his friends (verses 4 to 7)
In verses 4 to 7, Paul holds out the assurance to his readers that the peace of God will keep them in all the perplexities of life. In themselves, these perplexities offer little in the way of peace. But at

the end of the second millenium, life in terms of its stress points offers not many more solutions than life in Paul's day. People fall in and out of relationships, people experience unexpected loss, people struggle with economic deprivation, people unjustly suffer and die.

Even when the 'givens' of life are relatively stable and favourable, life at its spiritual core can be strangely empty and meaningless. As strange as it may seem in a culture like ours with so much to be enjoyed materially, there is often little sense of purpose or peace. That should not surprise us: inner peace is not contingent on external circumstances.

An elderly man I visited spoke about the disturbing trends he saw in today's society and then sadly added, 'I'm glad I'm going out, not coming in'. He'd lived through two world wars and coped, but now he felt he'd had enough: he was no longer at peace with the world, at least with his world. A similar anxiety afflicts many young people: the overall direction of the world, their prospects for the future, the lack of any sense of purpose for their lives all often lead to confusion and anxiety. Many people feel the same way.

In verse 7, Paul proclaims and promises peace, not as some escapist 'O for the wings of a dove' type of fantasy, but rather as a power to hold and sustain us in the midst of pressure and the disquiets of life.

There was once a Chinese painting competion to

illustrate the concept of peace. All the various entries came in: endless scenes of tranquil lakes, sunsets and landscapes, flowers and still lifes. But the winning entry saw something different. The artist pictured a storm with the bough of a tree bent almost double in the gale. The clouds poured out their fury and the tree seemed about to blow away. And there in the fork of the branch was a nest and inside the nest sat a bird, its wing sheltering its chick. Peace.

Similarly, what gives these words their irrepressible power is the *context* in which they are written. Paul wrote from prison. Perhaps he did not expect to see freedom again. Recently, he had suffered physical deprivation; he had been attacked; the integrity of his life's work had been called in question by opponents. Added to this, his major human source of fellowship and support, the church he loved, was bitterly divided by dispute and wrangling. And in all of that, he still talked of peace!

But the peace he talked about is the peace of God. And Paul made it clear that the peace of God is nothing other than the presence of God in the midst of any situation. God's presence has the potential not magically to change the situation, but enable us to perceive the situation differently and find a creative path through it. He works to make things good.

A good illustration of this is Paul's reaction to being in prison — a considerable frustration for a dynamic evangelist like Paul. Perhaps, but his reaction in verses 12 and 13 was very different. He knew that Christ was in the prison with him, the gospel was being spread and the church being built up and encouraged. Little wonder that Paul knew he did not need to fret!

Or consider the divisions in the church: he urged Euodia and Syntyche to agree in the Lord (chapter 4, verse 2). But God was there in the conflict; they could learn to 'agree in the Lord'.

Acts 15 provides a useful illustration of the same point. There, the church was struggling to see if there were special terms and conditions for Gentiles who became Christians. As they argued the point, the early Christians came to see that at every stage of the process that had led to the admission of Gentiles as full and equal members in Christ, God had been at work — leading, prompting, challenging and sometimes disturbing the status quo — to advance his purpose. The church was divided, but God was there amid the divisions — and the Christian could know his peace.

There are lessons for us in this early Christian experience. Disturbances in our lives may often be made good things: creative moments when we are challenged to see some new truth, to hear some new call, to take up some hitherto unattempted challenge. When I sang in the Choir of Trinity College, Glasgow, Professor William Barclay used to include regularly in our repertoire a song which said:

142/The bonds of faith

> It is God who is always driving a man
> to care about the coming day;
> And yet God is the mystery who takes
> each man's security away;
> It is God who is always driving us,
> for our work on earth is never done,
> It is God who gives every man his life,
> and God who takes his life away.

All of this is God at work. We can know his peace in the midst of life's perplexities.

Like the apostle's faith, the faith of German theologian Dietrich Bonhoeffer shone brightly against the darkness of imprisonment. Although often credited with (or blamed for!) being the inspiration behind the movement known as 'secular Christianity', Bonhoeffer was, to the end, a man of deep faith and prayer, as this excerpt from one of his letters shows. The letter is dated 21 August 1944, eight months before his death at the hands of his Nazi captors:

> All that we rightly expect from God and pray for is to be found in Jesus Christ... We must persevere in quiet meditation on the life, sayings, deeds, suffering and death of Jesus in order to learn what God promises and what he fulfils. One thing is certain: we must always live close to the presence of God, for things are possible with God; no earthly power can touch us

without his will, and danger can only drive us closer to him. We can claim nothing for ourselves, and yet we may pray for everything. Our joy is hidden in suffering, our life in death. But all through we are sustained in a wondrous fellowship. To all this God in Jesus has given us his Yea and Amen, and that is the firm ground on which we stand.[32]

Outwardly, his situation was bleak, but inwardly there was the assurance of the presence of God and Bonhoeffer's belief in the power of God. He knew that nothing would happen that was outside of God's will and purpose for his life.

Peace, indeed!

That experience comes close to what Paul is offering his friends at Philippi when he holds before them the promise of the peace of God.

It will help us confirm the strength of the experience Paul sought to share with his friends at Philippi if we try to think how Paul could be so confident in making his assurance about the peace of God.

The key to Paul's meaning is found in his statement, 'The Lord is near' (verse 5). We can't be sure whether this refers to a belief in the second coming which Paul and the early church expected sooner rather than later, or to an awareness of the presence of the risen and exalted Christ which believers can experience through the Spirit and through prayer.

Many people believe that Paul may have intended both and was being deliberately ambiguous to generate maximum support for his confidence and assurance. Christ the exalted Lord is available from heaven to bless and to protect; the same Lord Jesus will one day return to be Lord of all and establish his kingdom of righteousness and peace.

Certainly, when we think about the peace of God and how we may be sure of it, both these points are valuable input. We can enjoy the peace of God through the assurance that he is indeed with us: he knows us, he understands us, he loves us, he is at work in our lives.

A famous Scottish preacher and expositor at the turn of the century, Principal Robert Rainey, expressed it this way: 'The way to be anxious about nothing is to be prayerful about everything.' Another earthy layman, converted at the height of an impressive commercial career, used to say: 'Whenever you're in a fix, remember Philippians 4: 6!' But what gives prayer its power is not the use of scripture as some kind of mantra, but the heart belief that God is in control and that his love, revealed in Jesus Christ, is still working God's purpose out in the world and in the lives of his people.

When Jesus left his disciples at the end of his ministry and life, he promised to be with them through the Holy Spirit whom he would send from the Father (John 14, verses 16 to 20; see Acts 1, verses

4 to 8). We are assured that Jesus wants to be with us to the end of time. This is the exalted, reigning Jesus who is available to us with the power of God's divine love. Encouragement, indeed!

So we need not be anxious, knowing that Jesus is Lord, exalted at God's right hand.

The pursuit of the excellent — and how to recognise it (verses 8 and 9)

These verses contain some advice on how to live, which the Apostle Paul gave to his friends at Philippi. It is remarkable advice because the circle of things which, Paul says, Christians are to ponder and allow to influence them is astonishingly wide. There is nothing specifically Christian or religious about the items on the list: 'whatever is true, whatever is honourable, whatever is just. . . pure. . . pleasing. . . excellent. . . worthy of praise. . .'

What Paul is saying here is that we can be enriched for our living and our believing by many things in the world — indeed, by anything in the world — if approached in the right spirit.

This should not be surprising. After all, it is God's world and Christians affirm Jesus is Lord of all the world, in line with the teaching of scripture. The prologue to John's Gospel declares: 'All things came into being through him, and without him not one thing came into being' (John 1, verse 3) and this is echoed in the letter to the Colossians:

'All things have been created through him and for him. He himself is before all things and in him all things hold together' (Colossians 1, verses 16 and 17).

This means that Christians may find help, instruction and inspiration from many areas of life. This is the approach which is used to convey much of the teaching of the Bible, as in Jeremiah's allegory of the potter (Jeremiah 18, verses 1 to 12) and the parables of Jesus. Indeed, Jesus was prepared to use quite surprising people or situations to convey religious truth, as his parables of the unust judge (Luke 18, verses 1 to 8) and the dishonest manager (Luke 16, verses 1 to 13) bear out. Thus, the strategy Paul is commending here is in line with the teaching method of Jesus.

Just how wide-ranging may be the circle of things with potential to influence us is illustrated by Michel Quoist in his book, *Prayers of Life*:

> If only we knew how to look at life as God sees it, we should realise that nothing is secular in the world, but that everything contributes to the building of the kingdom of God. . . If we knew how to look at life through God's eyes, we should see it as innumerable tokens of the love of the creator seeking the love of his creatures. The Father has put us into the world, not to walk through it with lowered eyes, but to search for him through things, events, people. Everything must reveal God to us.[33]

Among the things which Quoist finds capable of revealing God, and around which he frames his meditative prayers, are the telephone, green blackboards, the wire fence, the tractor — even the pornographic magazine, hunger and a drunk man!

'Everything must reveal God to us.' That thought provides Christians with the incentive to explore the world of the arts and culture and find there things that are 'true... honourable... just ... pure... pleasing... commendable... excellent ... worthy of praise' (verse 8). By thinking on these things (and Paul means more than giving them a casual thought — he means we are to ponder, reflect on, even evaluate them), we will find our lives deepened and enriched.

Literature provides a good example. Its power to educate and enrich our lives illustrates Paul's point. Alexander Solzhenitsyn actually set out the value of literature along these lines in his 1970 Nobel Prize speech, *One Word of Truth*. He wrote:

> Art and literature can perform the miracle of overcoming man's characteristic weakness of learning only from his own experience, so that the experience of others passes him by. Art extends each man's short time on earth by carrying from man to man the whole complexity of other men's lifelong experience, with all its burdens, colours and flavour. Art re-creates in the flesh all

experience lived by other men, so that each man can make this his own.[34]

Michael Malone, the contemporary American novelist, supports this approach. He says of the task of writing:

> The core of fiction is always to get at mystery. Together we are all reading the mystery of God's plot. We are reading for clues to our connectedness to God, to the world — most of all to each other.[35]

As a sample of what he means, here is his description of the citizens of Dingley Falls reading at home, to be found in his story 'James':

> At night when the gutsy flotsam of life had settled, and the ghosts of the day sprang up grinning in the windows unseen, the readers of Dingley Falls read on. They read not merely to keep their eyes lowered so that they don't see the goblins. . . No, Dingleyans were reading because, unlike God and unlike the periscopes made by Dingley Optical Instruments, they could not see around corners; because from any one perspective life is so much less full than fiction and so much more painful. Safe in fiction, they were testing their hearts.[36]

The same holds true of music. Michael Leunig

has expressed the significant part music can play in enriching us in this prayer which he offered in thanksgiving for Mozart:

> We give thanks for the life and work of Wolfgang Amadeus Mozart. Let us celebrate and praise all those musicians and composers who give their hands and hearts and voices to the expression of life's mystery and joy. Who nourish our heart in its yearning. Who dignify our soul in its struggling. Who harmonise our grief and gladness. Who make melody from the fragments of chaos. Who align our spirits with creation. Who reveal to us the grace of God. Who calm us and delight us and set us free to love and forgive. Let us give thanks and rejoice. Amen.[37]

Some people might hesitate to see an artist such as Mozart as a vehicle of divine grace. The argument would be that, although his music is superb, what is now widely known of his life and behaviour would destroy any possibility that he could be thought of as an agent of God's grace. And, of course, Peter Schaffer's play and subsequent film, *Amadeus*, have made such behaviour very widely known. However, Jesus' use of unlikely characters to highlight God's grace encourages another look.

Commenting on the play, Samuel Terrien has written:

...the title is *Amadeus*, a name which suggests 'the gift of God, the love of God, the one whom God loves'. Mozart's genius is God's gift, undeserved, unmerited, totally inexplicable...[38]

It is a short step from thoughts such as those to the reflections of a grateful believer on the undeserved nature of God's grace experienced in salvation through Christ, as expressed in Ephesians 2, verses 8 and 9:

For by grace you have been saved through faith, and this is not your own doing; it is the gift of God — not the result of works, so that no-one may boast...

So even unlikely candidates may become channels of grace! On a different tack, I would also want to include within the remit of Paul's advice the contemplation of nature. Admittedly, it often appears as 'Nature red in tooth and claw', as Tennyson saw. But it is also the source of inexhaustible wonder and grace for those who pause to observe and reflect.

This is finely expressed in these lines from Mary Gilmore's poem, 'Of Wonder':

Give life its full domain and feed the soul
With wonder, find within a clod a world
Or, gazing on the rounded dewdrop purled

Upon a leaf, mark how its tiny bowl
Includes the sun...[39]

John Austen Baker goes so far as to complain that there are people who 'think of [God] as a God without joy' and who 'forgot that God could be happy'. He goes on:

> As for a universal openness to joy and beauty, such as the creator might be supposed to have had in making the universe at all, this perhaps has never been a characteristic of many men and women in any generation. As human beings, it is true, we do need something to be happy about; but there is no reason why the list of things that can make us glad should be so limited. Convention, prejudice, weariness, preoccupation with our own troubles, desire for the security of the familiar, narrow down and down, as the years go by, the scope of our joys and admirations. To walk down the street with God, then, would be an unnerving experience — 'You don't mean to say that you find that "very good"?'[40]

Baker's allusion there to the creation story in Genesis 1 is helpful: 'God saw everything that he had made, and indeed, it was very good' (Genesis 1, verse 31). This supplies the basic presupposition behind Paul's advice: it is God's world and God has blessed it with common grace, so that anything in it may teach us about God, or ourselves. Neither Christians nor the church have a monopoly on goodness or truth. While we may accept that statement as in principle true, we must also realise its implications and be open to as wide a circle of influence as possible.

This coincides with what Paul had said in Romans: God has given some revelation of himself in creation (Romans 1, verses 18 and 19) and even people outside of the community of faith may still do what the law of Moses commanded (Romans 2, verses 14 and 15). An extension of this thinking may be seen in Luke's account of Paul's preaching at Athens (Acts 17, verse 28), where Paul quotes from a Greek poet and philosopher to support the message of his address. Christians do not have a monopoly on truth: 'Everything must reveal God to us.'

At this point, however, it would be wise to enter a note of caution. Paul is not advocating that we should be completely undiscriminating in what we use. Not at all: however wide the circle may be of people or things which influence us, our centre must be fixed — on Christ, who is alone the truth and the measure of all truth. Paul makes precisely that point in verse 9, when he says:

> Keep on doing the things that you have learned and received and heard and seen in me, and the God of peace will be with you.

These words also open the believer to Christian sources of influence and guidance which are helpful in the business of living. The first of these is the Christian tradition or, if you like, Christian doctrine. Paul alludes to that when he talks about 'the things you have learned and received'.

The word 'learned' reminds us that one of the basic hallmarks of the early Christian church was what John Calvin called the 'teachable spirit'. The New Testament is full of it. Luke's summary of the life of the earliest community contains the detail that 'they devoted themselves to the apostles' teaching. . .' (Acts 2, verse 42) and among the gifts of the Holy Spirit which were experienced in the church was the gift 'that some should be. . . teachers' (Ephesians 4, verse 11). 1 Thessalonians 2, verse 9 onwards clearly show that a central feature of the life of the early church was teaching in the truths and duties of the Christian way. As we will see in a moment, Paul could even talk of 'my ways in Christ Jesus'.

The word 'received' is a word which Paul uses in reference to receiving Christian tradition, the central truths of the Christian faith. He uses it twice in 1 Corinthians of receiving the tradition about communion (1 Corinthians 11, verse 23) and the Easter proclamation of the church (chapter 15, verse 3). So, in addition to all our other reading and listening, we dare not neglect our Bibles in our thinking on what is true, honourable, just and so on.

Christ and Christian doctrine are given to measure, modify or amend all we see, hear and learn from God's world.

The Philippians also have the example of the apostle to guide and direct their thinking and actions. As we saw earlier (in chapter 3, verse 17), Paul is not afraid to point to his own conduct as a role model for Christian living and even to urge his readers to imitate him. This is not boasting; it is the confidence of the believer who knows that it is God who produces good works in our lives through the Spirit (as Ephesians 2, verse 10 states).

For Paul, consistency between word and deed, lesson and practice was essential and the measure of the consistency was Jesus Christ. Christian life and teaching centre on the Lord Jesus, and all the experiences of life are to be measured by reference to him. The circle of influence from which we learn may be wide, but the centre needs to be fixed on Christ. From this basis, then, the Christian knows how to approach the world of arts, culture and learning:

> Instead of destroying the arts or sciences or being indifferent to them, let us cultivate them with the enthusiasm of the (true) humanist, but at the same time consecrate them to the service of our God. Instead of stifling the pleasures afforded by the acquisition of knowledge, or by the appreciation of what is beautiful, let us accept these pleasures as the gifts of a heavenly Father.

Secure in her hold of Christ and his truth, the Christian is free to explore God's world and human culture with a lively interest and a sensitive, listening spirit, ready to put into practice the best of what she has learned.

Verses 8 and 9 is an affirming, positive statement about valuing whatever is good in God's creation. It is an appeal to turn away from rigid, censorious, fortress-like approaches to life. As Fred Craddock says, 'The church that takes a rigid, over-against-the-world posture is now and again forced to go in search of a more adequate theology.'[42]

Springtime for the church (verses 10 to 21)

The late Sammy Davis Jr used to sing: 'If I ruled the world, every day would be the first day of spring. . .'

This is an interesting image. The 'first day of spring' is not always the day of romantic beauty and sunshine that the popular mythology of the song would make out; in reality, it can often be cold and wet! Despite that, I find the first day of spring very special, almost an exciting day. Even if it is still winter, for those in the more temperate climates of the globe it is a day full of the promise of things to come.

I mention this because of Paul's words to the Philippians in verse 10. His friends, who had previously supported his mission work generously but who had, for some reason unknown to us, ceased to do so, suddenly started up their support once more, sending a generous gift with Epaphroditus to support his work.

As he wrote to thank them, Paul was caught up in the significance of their gift.

'You have revived your concern for me' (verse 10) literally means 'your care for me has blossomed afresh'. It is a unique expression in the New Testament, filled with poetic boldness and vivid descriptive power. It's as though he'd said, 'With this gift, you have made it the first day of spring. All the promise of summer with its warmth, colour and growth is there for me. Thank you!' The season of spring is an apt perspective through which to view the expression of Christian faith which any such Christian giving represents.

Paul expresses this thought even though there is a part of him which is embarrassed by the gift. Indeed, he did not want the gift. Paul liked to be independent in his ministry — dependent on no-one, so that he might be accused by no-one and accountable to no-one. . . but God.

He is particularly prickly about this in his letters to the Corinthians, brought out well in 2 Corinthians 11, verses 7 onwards. So far as we know, the church at Philippi was the only one he allowed to share in his work in this way. That's why there is a note of personal embarrassment detectable in this thankyou letter. To be sure, Paul covered his embarrassment well, indicating that as a servant of Christ he is able to 'make do' in whatever circumstances life threw up at him (and we know from 2 Corinthians 11, verses 23 to 33 just how tough some of those circumstances had been for Paul).

Interestingly, he began by talking about being self-sufficient, but soon corrected this into being sufficient 'through Christ who gives me strength' (verse 13). Even so, there was much about this support that Paul could genuinely appreciate.

For instance, he knew that the giving was not just a gift to him; it was also a gift to God and an expression of the commitment of his friends at Philippi to the extension of the kingdom of God. He described it in verse 18 in a way which lifts the question of Christian giving to new heights.

'A fragrant offering' is language that occurs also in Ephesians 5, verse 2. Here, it is used of Jesus and his death: 'Christ loved us and gave himself for us, a fragrant offering and sacrifice to God.' It's as though he said that *any* offering, even the gift of money, reflects Christ's offering of himself to God and that any sacrifice becomes identified with Christ's sacrifice on our behalf.

We know that's true at the basic level — money for Christian causes promotes Christian work. But here the spiritual significance of such offering is made clear.

Giving for God's work is not looked upon by Paul lightly or as a matter of our preference or convenience: it is fundamental to faith and connects us closely with Christ in his death. It is nothing less than part of our giving of ourselves to God. And the point Paul makes here applies equally to us: every time we give, faith 'blossoms' again — it is springtime for the church.

That is why, even with his embarrassment, Paul cannot conceal his joy at the Philippians' gift. Their giving had made it, for Paul, the first day of spring: there is the promise of warmth and growth in the air.

The warmth, of course, is the warmth of genuine Christian fellowship. Remember, Paul is in prison: there is the likelihood that he will not get out again. But he is not alone. He is caught up in a fellowship of love, concern and common commitment to Christ. It is hard to exaggerate the value of the support this would have brought Paul — or its importance for us today.

In the work of the church overseas, as in the work of the church at home, our giving allows ministry in Christ's name to be brought to people in their need. Many of the people the church seeks to reach have reached the end of their tether. But they can be told they are not alone, there is someone who cares, and there is in Jesus someone greater who cares — whose love and power can make everything new. The warmth of that Christian love can bring hope and life again to people in their struggle.

And in the springtime of the church there is growth: Paul knows his own life's work may be over — but God's work goes on. It does not all depend on him, however dedicated and enthusiastic he may be. The Philippians' money made possible further ministry: Epaphroditus (first referred to in chapter 2, verses 25 onwards and now in verse 18), who had brought their gift, had also worked for Paul to carry on his ministry. Who knows what lives were touched and healed as a result?

The German theologian Dorothee Soelle wrote:

> Church . . .resides not in us alone; we have brothers and sisters who help us in life. . .
> Precisely because we recognise that our own lives, isolated and separated from others, are barren and insufficient, we have therefore linked ourselves up with the desires, the courage and the work of the many.[43]

Our giving is part of that linking up which Soelle mentions: when we give, we empower others for service. We may not always see the end result of what we do; we may not always know the growth which God makes possible. What we do know is that both the growth and the fruits of that growth will be there by the power of God.

That reflects one dimension of the truth of what Paul had stated in chapter 1, verse 6: 'I am confident of this, that the one who began a good work among you will bring it to completion by the day of Jesus.'

Farewell! (verses 21 to 23)

In the English language, the words we use when parting from someone have become curiously devalued. We say 'Goodbye' with scarcely a thought that the word is an abbreviation for an expression originally much more significant: 'God be with you.' Equally, 'Farewell' is a wish or a prayer: 'May you fare well, may you succeed.'

Ancient Greek seems to have had a similar problem of devaluation. Its word of farewell, *chaire*, means literally 'rejoice' and implies the prayer, 'May you go on your way rejoicing.' (Incidentally, one of the problems affecting the unity of the letter is that at the start of Philippians 3, verse 1, Paul appears to be saying farewell — although this is disguised by many modern translations which render along the lines of 'I wish you all joy in the Lord.')

Anyway, although he does not use the actual word normally translated 'farewell' at the conclusion of the letter, Paul still in effect bids his friends at Philippi farewell. What he really means is farewell in the deeper, richer sense: 'May you fare well.'

In verse 21, he sends his greetings to 'each one of God's people'. As this translation makes clear, this greeting is couched in the singular — as if Paul wanted to emphasise that each individual member of the church was included. That was a wise strategy for a church which had problems caused by leaders disagreeing (chapter 4, verses 1 to 3) and whose members Paul frequently had to encourage to work together in unity of purpose (as in chapter 1, verse 27 and chapter 2, verses 1 to 4). In such an atmosphere, mention of any individuals could prove invidious and collective greetings might do nothing to encourage unity. Perhaps that is why the singular is used here.

Paul is always concerned that Christians work together. And it goes almost without saying, this is absolutely necessary if any church or fellowship is to flourish in our own day.

In verse 22, he passes on the greetings of the Christians in whose city he is imprisoned, including the tantalising reference to 'particularly those of the emperor's household'. Certainly, it is possible to take these words literally to mean the family of the emperor; it is much more probable that the reference is, as the REB translation of the Bible makes clear, to 'those in the emperor's service' — probably meaning members of the imperial civil service. It is possible that the presence of such people among the Christians sending greetings to Philippi is the result of the 'progress of the gospel' Paul mentioned in chapter 1, verses 12 to 14.

It is a great encouragement to any Christian group to see the gospel effect change in the lives of people, gathering new converts into the community of God's people. If the Philippians were able to realise that Gentiles were coming to faith in Christ even in the face of difficulties such as Paul's imprisonment, they would find encouragement to continue their own task.

Finally, there is a prayer (verse 23) for Christ's grace to be with his friends. Here again, Paul made a subtle linguistic point. He wrote, 'The grace. . . be with your [plural] spirit [singular].' It is almost as though he wanted to emphasise that the believers at Philippi, 'though many, are one body' (1 Corinthians 12, verse 12).

Paul's letter began with the greeting, 'grace and peace' (chapter 1, verse 2). It now closes with a prayer for 'the grace of the Lord Jesus Christ', which Paul knows is always available and (as chapter 4, verse 19 suggests) never exhaustible. As Christians rely on grace, they can only *fare well*!

In reflecting on the emphasis on Jesus' grave at the end of the letter, Karl Barth brings out the two features he feels are strongest in the book, one relating to the life of the believer, the other to Jesus' death for us:

> So the letter ends with the same objectivity and superiority with which it began, and in which it is at once both one of the most remarkable

evidences of how human a Christian can be and a testimony to an event which can only be designated as the very limit of what is understood by human history.[44]

Philippians allows a glimpse of how human a Christian Paul could be — and, for that matter, the Christians at Philippi, although Barth makes no reference to them! It is true that the apostle gives evidence of a faith which is in some ways stronger than many contemporary Christians might be able to express — for example, in his refusal to be rattled by the false motives of the competing preachers (in chapter 1, verses 17 and 18), or in his desire 'to depart and be with Christ' (in chapter 1, verse 23).

Nonetheless, the letter leaves us with the abiding impression of a Christian caught up in the frailty and vulnerability of the church. There are fightings without (chapter 3, verse 28 refers to 'your opponents') and divisions within (such as in chapter 2, verse 21; chapter 3, verse 1 following — 'the dogs . . . the evilworkers' — and chapter 4, verses 2 to 4). Paul feels the need to issue calls to humility (chapter 2, verses 1 to 11) and to unity (chapter 1, verses 27 to 30; chapter 2, verses 3, 4 and 14) which point to problems in the fellowship of the church.

Paul himself has to face the possibility of imminent death (chapter 1, verses 22 to 23 and chapter 2, verse 17) and shows the vacillation which most of us experience in time of crisis (chapter 1, verse 23). In addition, there is the tension he feels in the face of the normal human anxieties brought on by the ill-health of loved ones, as in chapter 2, verses 25 and following. A very human scenario, indeed!

Alongside of that frailty, however, the letter demands that we set firmly in place the reality of the Christian faith and observe its power to hold and sustain all who put their faith in Jesus Christ. Christ and his self-giving love are the models for Christian behaviour (chapter 2, verses 4 to 11). 'Christ and the power of his resurrection' (chapter 3, verse 10) shine through at every point in the letter, overcoming difficulties and creating faith (chapter 4, verse 13), hope (chapter 3, verses 10 and 11) and peace (chapter 4, verse 7; compare verse 10).

As Paul addresses the particular situation of his readers out of the particular situation he faces, he finds an answer in Christ: 'My God will supply every need of yours according to his riches in glory in Christ Jesus' (chapter 4, verse 19). This is the appropriate testimony of a life lived in such a way that 'Christ is proclaimed in every way... and in that I rejoice' (chapter 1, verse 18), 'for to me, living is Christ' (chapter 1, verse 21).

Thus the apostle allows us to observe the persistence of faith — in his own life and in the lives of some of his friends and colleagues — in spite of many difficulties and disappointments. His faith encourages him to make the unqualified promise that 'the peace of God which surpasses all understanding will guard your hearts and minds in Christ Jesus' (chapter 4, verse 7).

Contemporary Christians who nourish their faith with the teaching of this letter will discover, in their own lives too, that their faith not only persists, but can sustain them through every difficulty and disappointment, and bring inner peace amid any outer chaos.

Discussion questions

Talking it through

1 What is the peace of God? If it doesn't do away with our problems, what does it do?

2 Availing ourselves of the power and presence of God is an effective antidote to stress and worry. Describe a recent experience where prayer *to* God (verse 6) has brought you the peace *of* God (verse 7).

Was Paul's testimony — that his heart and mind were 'guarded' — true for you?

3 The 'pursuit of excellence' has become a passion for business managers and consultants. How can we put this on our personal agenda as part of our character formation? See verse 8.

4 'Content with whatever I have' (verse 11). How is this good advice to yuppies, DINKS (double income — no kids) and other contemporary materialists? How are our wants different from our needs? What does God promise us? See verses 12, 13 and 19.

5 Paul wasn't ashamed to accept money from his fellow Christians, even though he did not actively seek it (verse 17). How did he view such gifts (verse 18)? What should be the attitude of the giver (verses 15 and 16)?

Are there rules for discerning the sham operator from the legitimate Christian worker in financial need?

Widening our horizons

1 'I'm glad I'm not growing up in today's world.'
Is change necessarily something to be frightened of? Look at change in each of the following areas and suggest how 'the peace of God' could influence our attitude to it:
(a) the trend from full-time to part-time and other flexible work arrangements
(b) the challenge to traditional husband-wife roles in the family
(c) the growth of alternative religious traditions generally (pluralism).

2 Apply the words of chapter 4, verse 8 to the following activities:
(a) the selection of suitable films and videos
(b) the use of our money
(c) the apportioning of our leisure time.

3 What case would you make out for giving financial support to each of the following:
(a) sponsorship of a Third World child through an aid agency?
(b) gifts of food to an aid agency caring for homeless people in our cities?
(c) financial support for your local church?

(d) providing free accommodation in your home for a needy family?
(e) contributing capital to a new business venture undertaken by someone you believe in?

Resources are finite. What principles would you use in apportioning your gifts?

4 Author Charles Ringma writes: 'Community is not built by wishful thinking. It is not achieved by dreaming. It does not come about simply by longing for a place of friendship, meaningful relationships and solidarity. Neither is community achieved only by prayer. Community, that fragile gift of commonality, is built on deeds. It comes about when people are prepared to love and serve each other' (*Dare to Journey with Henri Nouwen*, Albatross, 1992).

Discuss this statement in the light of the way the Philippian church lived and acted.

5 After completing reading and discussing the letter to the Philippians, what would be your preferred practical response:
(a) going for a quiet walk?
(b) taking positive action on some key issue, e.g. writing a letter to a friend?
(c) praying about a specific issue?

Endnotes

1. Fred Craddock, *Philippians*, John Knox, 1985, p.2
2. The order of events can be worked out from Philippians 4, verse 15 onwards; 2 Corinthians 11, verse 8; Acts 19, verse 22; and Acts 20, verse 1 onwards.
3. Acts 23, verse 33; Acts 26, verse 32; Acts 28, verses 14 to 31
4. Philippians 4, verse 15; Philippians 2, verses 19, 23–24, 26 and 28
5. Philippians 1, verse 12
6. Romans 15, verse 22 onwards; Philippians 1, verse 25; Philippians 2, verse 24
7. Philippians 1, verse 19 onwards; Philippians 4, verse 13
8. Philippians 2, verses 1 to 5; Philippians 4, verse 10 onwards; Philippians 2, verses 12 to 18
9. F.W. Beare, *The Epistle to the Philippians*, Adam and Charles Black, 1969, p.2
10. Viktor E. Frankl, *Man's Search for Meaning*, Simon and Schuster, 1963, p.127
11. Karl Barth, *Letters 1961–1968*, Eerdmans, 1981, p.259
12. Fred Craddock, *ibid*, p.14
13. Fred Craddock, *ibid*, p.21
14. Anonymous, in Mary Craig, *Blessings*, Hodder and

Stoughton, 1979, p.136
15. Fred Craddock, *ibid*, p.26
16. Michael Bourdeaux, *Risen Indeed: Lessons in Faith from the USSR*, Darton, Longman & Todd, 1983, p.59
17. Fred Craddock, *Luke*, John Knox Press, 1990, p.259
18. Hans Kung, *On Being a Christian*, Edward Quinn (tr.), Collins, 1977, p.126
19. Eric James, *A Life of Bishop John A.T. Robinso:n: Scholar, Pastor, Prophet*, Collins, 1987, p.309
20. David H.C. Read, *Grace Thus Far*, Eerdmans, 1986, p.49
21. F.W. Beare, *ibid*, p.29
22. Fred Craddock, *ibid*, p.43
23. Fred Craddock, *ibid*, p.42
24. Arthur C. Cochrane, *The Church's Confession under Hitler*, Westminster Press, 1982, p.240
25. Jim Wallis, *The Call to Conversion*, Lion, 1981, pp.18–19
26. Gonville A. Ffrench-Beytagh, *Encountering Darkness*, Collins, 1973, pp.161–162
27. Gerald F. Hawthorne, *Philippians*, Word, 1983, p.131
28. In *Uniting in Worship*, Uniting Church in Australia, Assembly Commission on Liturgy, Melbourne, Joint Board of Religious Education, 1988
29. Alexander Solzhenitsyn, *Stories and Prose Poems*, Michael Glenny (tr.), Penguin, 1973, p.204
30. Count Nikolaus von Zinzendorf's story can be found in John Stott, *Focus on Christ*, Collins Fount, 1979, p.136 onwards
31. Karl Barth, *ibid*, p.4
32. Dietrich Bonhoeffer, *Letters and Papers from Prison*, Collins Fontana, 1959, p.130
33. Michel Quoist, *Prayers of Life*, Logos Books, 1963, pp.10
34. Alexander Solzhenitsyn, *One Word of Truth*, Nobel Speech on Literature, The Bodley Head, 1972, p.14.

This and other uses of non-inclusive language are products of their age, not ours. They are included here in the hope that such language does not detract from the otherwise valuable nature of the material.

35. Cited in Donald W. McCulloch, 'What does Literature have to do with Ministry?' in *Theology, News & Notes*, XXXVIII, 2 (December 1991), Pasadena CA, 3.

36. *op.cit*, in *Incarnation — Contemporary Writers on the New Testament*, Alfred Corn (ed.), Viking, 1990, pp.301–302

37. Michael Leunig, *The Prayer Tree*, Collins Dove, 1991, fourth prayer

38. Samuel Terrien, 'Amadeus Revisited', in *Theology Today*, XLII 4 (January 1988), Princeton NJ, p.438

39. *op.cit*, in *A Book of Australian Verse*, Judith Wright (ed.), Oxford University Press, 1968, p.58

40. John Austen Baker, *The Foolishness of God*, Collins Fontana, 1970, p.389f.

41. Gresham Macken, 'Christianity and Culture', in *Banner of Truth Magazine*, Banner of Truth, June 1989, p.18

42. Fred Craddock, *ibid*, p.73

43. Dorothee Soelle, 'Church: They had Everything in Common', in *Theology Today*, XLII 2 (July 1985), p.218

44. Karl Barth, *The Epistle to the Philippians*, SCM, 1962, comments on chapter 4, verses 10 to 23

Bibliography

Useful commentaries on Philippians

Karl Barth, *The Epistle to the Philippians*, SCM, 1962
A short commentary with some valuable insights.

F.W. Beare, *The Epistle to the Philippians*, in *Black's New Testament Commentaries*, Adam and Charles Black, 1969
A commentary that provides practical insights to the text.

F.F. Bruce, *Philippians*, in the *New International Bible Commentary* series, Hendrickson, 1989
Useful for both the scholar and the general reader.

Fred Craddock, *Philippians, Interpretation: A Bible Commentary for Teaching and Preaching*, John Knox, 1985
Provides not only exegesis, but a number of valuable applications to church and society today.

Gerald F. Hawthorn, *Philippians*, Word, 1983
A detailed exegesis of the Greek text.

Ralph Martin, *Philippians*, in the *New Century Bible Commentary* series, Marshall, Morgan and Scott, 1982
A reliable, detailed commentary.

Peter O'Brien, *Commentary on Philippians*, Eerdmans, 1991
A detailed, scholarly, exegetical treatment of the Greek text — the most recent commentary to be published.

Useful treatments of key ideas in Philippians

Robert Banks, *Paul's Idea of Community*, Lancer, 1987
The author draws out the socially distinctive ideas and practices of the churches in the Greek cities, including Philippi, in Paul's day.

Gunther Bornkamm, *Paul*, Hodder and Stoughton, 1990
A scholarly look at the apostle's gospel and theology, confirming that Paul was attuned to the mind of Jesus.

Ronald Brownrigg, *Pauline Places*, Hodder and Stoughton, 1989
Using plenty of illustrated material, this book follows in the footsteps of Paul.

John Temple Bristow, *What Paul Said About Women*, Harper, 1991
Makes out a strong case for equality of the sexes, dealing with the key passages in Philippians.

Useful treatments of present-day faith-and-life issues raised in Philippians

John Allen, John Butterworth and Myrtle Langley, *A Book of Beliefs*, Lion, 1981
A wide-ranging introduction to the great religions, cults, faiths and mysteries of the world today.

Robert Banks, *All the Business of Life*, Albatross, 1987
Sets out to bridge the gap between belief and the activities of everyday life.

Robert and Julia Banks, *The Church Comes Home: A New Base for Community and Mission*, Albatross, 1989
Looks at the church in the home today, reflecting many of the problems and rewards of the Philippian church.

Dietrich Bonhoeffer, *Life Together*, SCM, 1954
The outline of a communal life based on Jesus' principles — a modern-day classic.

José Comblin, *Cry of the Oppressed, Cry of Jesus*, Orbis, 1984
An examination of the situation and requirements of the poor throughout history and today.

Donald Dorr, *Integral Christianity*, Collins Dove, 1990
How prayer can integrate community, justice and peace issues.

Thomas Fenton and Mary Heffron, *Third World Struggle for Peace and Justice*, Orbis, 1990
A list of resources for those working through this issue.

Richard Foster, *Money, Sex and Power*, Hodder and Stoughton, 1985
Outlines the biblical principles that can enable us to live out a truly Christian response to these three issues.

Art Gish, *Living in Christian Community*, Albatross, 1980
An outline of some principles that can be used in establishing Christian community today.

Hans Kung, *On Being a Christian*, Edward Quinn (tr.), Collins, 1977
A powerful explication by the Dutch Catholic theologian of what it means to be a Christian at the end of the twentieth century, being true to the teachings of Jesus, yet in touch with contemporary society.

Ronald Sider, *Rich Christians in an Age of Hunger*, Hodder and Stoughton, 1977
A biblical response to the need to face the issues of world poverty and affluence.

John Taylor, *Enough is Enough*, SCM, 1975
An outline of principles behind the need to avoid excess and give to the poor.

Jean Vanier, *The Broken Body: Journey to Wholeness*, Paulist Press
The author looks at the meaning of Jesus, the obedient sufferer, for today.